BREAK EVERY YOKE

BREAK EVERY YOKE

CHRISTIAN HELP FOR HALFWAY HOUSES AND THE HOMELESS

BY DR. TIM LANIGAN
WITH A FOREWORD BY PASTOR MARK SWIGER

Charleston, SC
www.PalmettoPublishing.com

Break Every Yoke
Copyright © 2020 by Tim Lanigan

Unless otherwise indicated, all Scripture quotations are taken from the New King James Version®. Copyright © 1982 by Thomas Nelson. Used by permission. All rights reserved.

Scripture quotations marked (ERV) are taken from the The Prison Bible: Easy-to-Read Version (ERV), International Edition © 2013, 2016 by Bible League International and used by permission.

Unless otherwise indicated, italic words or phrases in quotations are added by the author, and all photos taken by Tim Lanigan
Photo of the author taken by Robert J. Boynton, Jr., maker of the oxen yoke
Man on the cover: Dan Fichera

Paperback ISBN: 978-1-63837-013-0
Hardcover ISBN: 978-1-64990-409-6
eBook ISBN: 978-1-64990-410-2

For our family: Daniel, Colleen, her husband Michael, Bonnie, her husband Andy, and Frank; our grandkids Olivia, Joshua, Isaiah, and Chloe.

TABLE OF CONTENTS

FOREWORD

The author of this book, Tim, graciously considers me to be one of his mentors, but I would be hard pressed to say which one of us has benefitted more. He is not only successful in his own calling and ministry but is also a faithful partner in the work I do (and several other ministries). I believe one of the greatest signs of Christian maturity is to care more about others than you do about yourself. If you meet Tim, he will not want to talk about himself. He genuinely wants to know about you. He is looking to see if he can help you in some way. If you could listen to his heart speak you would hear: "Lord... I feel your love for this person...How can I help them find the joy and success in life you want them to have?"

It is in this Spirit this book has been written. It is actually an expression of the cry of God's heart. Tim has heard that cry and responded by letting God speak through him. You see, the Lord is looking for people to fill a great need in this hour. This book is actually a posting in the "Help Wanted" section of heaven's newspaper. God wants your help. God is still setting the captives free. Prisoners are being released back into society at record numbers. God needs people to love them and meet the many practical and spiritual needs arising from their release. One of the many startling statistics that Tim lists in this book is that two thousand prisoners are being sent back into society every day. That's 730,000 people every year. I realized that if God used someone to help 10 prisoners a year, it would mean He has 73,000 job openings where you can serve right now!

At this moment there are hundreds of thousands of believers sitting in churches. Each has their own personal set of problems and concerns. Many are "stuck" – no longer growing or challenged in their walk with the Lord. The answer to this is found in the Bible: *"Look not every man on his own things, but every man also on the things of others"* Philippians 2:4.

To mature we must start caring more about others things more than our own things.

As you read this book you will hear the cry and concern of God's heart through Tim. It is his desire that many thousands will respond and answer that cry by starting new ministries in your area or plugging in to serve in an existing ministry. People are needed from every background…If you have skills or no skills… education or no education…you are needed.

Jesus said: "My sheep hear my voice". As you read this book listen for the voice of the Lord in these pages. If there is any desire in your heart to love and serve God I know you will be inspired and respond.

Mark Swiger, Founder and President,
Mark Swiger Ministries

(MARK SWIGER MINISTRIES, USED BY PERMISSION)

Mark and Paulette Swiger have served the Lord together for over 40 years. In 1996 they accepted a call to serve in the nations of the world, forming Mark Swiger Ministries, a non-profit 501(c)(3) Corporation dedicated to revealing the love and healing power of Jesus Christ to all people. Since that time, they have ministered on five continents of the world, preaching to millions of people face to face. They conducted more city-wide campaigns in India from 1996-2006 than any other international ministry. Mark is an ordained minister with the Assemblies of God and author of *Miracles and Multitudes: Secrets of the End-Time Harvest,* and *What is a Disciple and How Do You Make One? A Manual for Christian Pastors and Leaders.*

INTRODUCTION

A yoke, in its literal sense, is a harness for beasts of burden. It is basically a wooden crossbeam, usually having two bows or neck braces. Its purpose is to put beasts of burden to a task. The beasts put to the task are compelled by the whip and the left or right leaning of the yoke by the attached harness. There is a powerlessness, an inability to choose your own direction. When considered as a metaphor applied to humans, the imagery indicates abuse, addiction, brokenness, bondage, despair – each a form of oppression. In every corner of the world, people are being yanked around by yokes of oppression.

If you've been to an American State Fair, where there is typically an event called an oxen pull, you would have an opportunity to see oxen pairs from different farms compete in dragging a heavy load. These pairs of oxen are yoked together and prompted, positioned, and spurred on by a goad, or whip, together with the yelling of commands. They are connected to a sled, with increasing cement weights being added. When the harness ring is hitched onto the sled and the position of the oxen pair is just right, the driver whips and shouts commands for the pulling forward of the heavy sled as the oxen strain forward.

HOPKINTON, NEW HAMPSHIRE STATE FAIR,
2019 (PHOTO BY THE AUTHOR)

The symbolism of a yoke is seen throughout the Old and New Testaments. The specific phrase used as a title for this book, *Break Every Yoke*, is from Isaiah 58:6, in which God describes the kind of sacrifice or fast that He really wants from us, if we honestly want to give something up or respond to Him with our lives:

> Is this not the fast that I have chosen:
> To loose the bonds of wickedness,
> To undo the heavy burdens,
> To let the oppressed go free,
> And that you *break every yoke?* (Isaiah 58:6)

An extreme example of a yoke of oppression is the historic event, the centerpiece of history – Jesus carrying the cross. Both the crossbeam and the whip were used. Our Lord compels us to be concerned for the yoke of oppression. The phrase "loose the bonds of wickedness" literally means in Hebrew "undo the cords of the yoke." The term *yoke* is pronounced *motah* in Hebrew. The phrase *break every yoke* literally means "tear apart every yoke."

Bonds of wickedness and heavy burdens can be seen in many walks of life. They represent the front lines of Christian ministry. The two main areas of concern being considered for this book are

1. people in halfway houses newly released from prison, and
2. those without a home

These two groups have much in common, and there is an overlap of circumstances. Many former inmates are among the homeless, and many who have been released into a halfway house find themselves homeless. A yoke of oppression common to both groups is an overwhelming percentage of drug and alcohol addiction.

THE FORMER PRISONER

People are put into prison for two main purposes: to be punished for their crime and to undergo rehabilitation. There are some who see punishment as the sole reason for incarceration, having a "throw-away-the-key" perspective. There are others who emphasize the importance of rehabilitation, the intent of which is twofold. First, prisoners are rehabilitated so that they will avoid repeating the mistake of an offense. Second, rehabilitation helps to protect the public from that repeat offense. Opinions vary regarding the necessity and value of rehabilitation. The halfway house, however, is a pivotal test of the process of rehabilitation, along with being a stressful time of re-acclimation and re-engaging with family, friends, work, home, and life on the outside. It is a tough transition. State and Federal halfway houses exist as transitional housing for the former prisoner.

The statistics of incarceration are staggering. A wealth of information is available through the *Office of Justice Programs – Bureau of Justice Statistics* (www.ojp.usdoj.gov), and a helpful series of charts and diagrams are available through *The Sentencing Project* (sentencingproject.org). The state and federal prison population in the United States is over 1.57 million, and when considering the number of people in jails, it totals 2.2 million, which represents a rate of 716 prisoners per 100,000 people.[1] (With policy changes and non-violent prisoner releases the early rate for 2020 is 655 per 100,000).[2] This is the largest rate of incarceration in the world. "Sentencing policies of the War on Drugs era resulted in dramatic growth in incarceration for drug offenses... At the federal level, prisoners incarcerated on a drug conviction make up half the prison population. At the state level the number of drug offenders in prison has increased eleven-fold since 1980."[3] Racial disparity is strongly evident. "More than 60% of the people in prison today are people of color. Black men are six times more likely to be incarcerated than white men and 2.5 times more likely than

Hispanic men."[4] The lifetime likelihood of imprisonment for all U.S. men is 1 in 9, with white men 1 in 17, Latino men at 1 in 6, and black men at 1 in 3.[5] This disparity indicates a deep cultural problem, as does the extent of American incarceration itself. Life sentences (life without parole) have increased from 70,000 in 1992 to 160,000 in 2012, more than doubling in twenty years. As for juveniles in adult prisons and jails:

> There has been a troubling shift in the nation's responses to at-risk youth over the last 25 years. The creators of the juvenile justice system originally viewed it as a system for providing prevention, protection, and redirection to youth, but it is more common for youth today to experience tough sanctions and adult-type punishments instead. While reforms are underway in many jurisdictions, there remains an urgent need to reframe our responses to youth delinquency.[6]

Rehabilitation programs should be aggressively utilized, and with a contemporary climate of early release, the urgency of addressing reentry becomes more paramount.

The national recidivism rate is 67.8 percent for a three-year period, with a disappointing rate of 76.6 percent arrested within five years of release.[7] These recidivism rates are symptomatic of a failure of the prison systems to rehabilitate! Nationally, two out of three are rearrested after three years, and three out of four are reincarcerated after five years!

Three Out of Four *Return* to Prison Nationally!

Christian volunteers throughout the United States serve in prison ministries in different ways. Some preach during services in chapels; some mentor individuals; others are part of a team which provides transitional programs. One such program, The Authentic Christian Man, is a Christian discipleship ministry conducted by volunteers at the men's prison in Concord, New Hampshire, which I was part of for fifteen years. This inmate program involves weekly meetings for three months in the spring and fall, with teaching and small group conversation. Many of these former inmates have been released into the Calumet Transitional Housing Unit, which is their halfway house. During the small group conversations, we became aware of the nervousness evident among those who finally were granted their parole, as they were being released to the halfway house. They continue to be challenged with the hurdles of adjusting to reconnecting with families, finding work, and establishing homes.

Winds of change are blowing across the United States. Statistics of yesteryear may not apply to the near future. Police reform, prison policy, and law and order itself is in a state of upheaval and transition. Many more former prisoners are likely to find themselves in reentry into the general population. In other words, the needs and concerns pointed out throughout this book are becoming deeper and greater. For compassionate Christians, it is becoming a time for all hands on deck.

THE HOMELESS

The challenges of ex-prisoner reentry frequently result in the additional complication of homelessness. I encounter many people who are former inmates during conversations at 1269 Café, an outreach to the homeless. Pat Nolan writes,

> studies in New York City found that more than 30 percent of those entering its homeless shelters had recently been released from correctional institutions. A survey of Boston shelters found that nearly one-quarter of the released prison population experienced homelessness within a year of release; some were homeless immediately upon release, while others became homeless shortly thereafter, when temporary living situations dissolved.[8]

Boston is just fifty-two miles from Manchester, but these cities do not require proximity to share similar homelessness circumstances. These problems are shared by every major city in the United States. Mark P. Fisher writes, "On a single night in January

2017, the number of men, women and children in America experiencing homelessness was 564,000. Those could fill nearly 8 NFL stadiums."[9] Who knows the true accuracy of the extent of homelessness? Those who are not counted are difficult to count.

Since 2013, I have been an associate pastor with 1269 Café, which is an outreach ministry to the homeless in downtown Manchester, New Hampshire. This ministry has lunchtime meals, provides showers and laundry; hosts a Suboxone clinic, an Alpha program, and my own Recovery Bible Study (a 7-week series). The cafe offers a Sunday worship service with praise music, a sermon message, and a fellowship lunch. I will soon begin the Rebuilding Your Life Program there. Many former inmates attend 1269 Café.

MARY AND CRAIG CHEVALIER, FOUNDERS OF 1269 CAFÉ, AN OUTREACH TO THE HOMELESS

The troubles of the city of Manchester are reflected in the lives of the guests of 1269 Café and among those who are residents of the Helping Hands Outreach sober-living housing unit, where I have served as chaplain for three years. Located in an older brick building with thirty-five beds, there is accountability among the men, with urine testing and zero-tolerance for drug or alcohol use. If individuals are dismissed, they have an opportunity to return if they have undergone thirty days of rehab. Christian Aftercare Ministries deserves an honorable mention. It is an evangelistic outreach on behalf of the former prisoner and has an office in the "Good News Hallway" shared by the chaplain office in the Helping Hands building. Paul Roussel and Mike Grady of Christian Aftercare Ministries also volunteer at Valley Street Jail, the New Hampshire State Prison for Men in Concord, and at the Calumet Transitional Housing Unit, or halfway house just up the street. The majority of men coming to Helping Hands Outreach have been incarcerated, and many of them have arrived in a state of homelessness. The men of Calumet have all been released from prison, but homelessness looms in the future for many of them.

HELPING HANDS OUTREACH BUILDING,
MANCHESTER, NEW HAMPSHIRE

CASE MANAGER LICENSED ALCOHOL AND DRUG
COUNSELOR GUY TORGERSEN (LEFT) AND HELPING
HANDS OUTREACH DIRECTOR LARRY NICE

It is because of these troubles and in spite of them, that we are serving the Lord and ministering to these former prisoners, and in the case of 1269 Café, homeless men, women, and young ones. The need for counseling, coaching, mentoring, recovery encouragement, and Christian evangelism is strongly apparent. These transitional circumstances reflect a deep, profound need.

I have mentioned some of the local ministries in New Hampshire, U.S.A., to provide context for outreach which is ongoing. The needs of the former prisoner and the homeless are worldwide. Every city across the United States has people in need. *You can be instrumental in helping those who need to rebuild their lives in your local town or city.* I am also writing to people in my native country of Canada (born in New Brunswick), to distant relatives and the sports-loving folks of Australia and New Zealand, to extended family in Ireland, the rest of the British Isles, the nations of Europe, Asia, Africa, and South America.

The Christian believer operates within the biblical worldview which holds high regard for the characteristic of forgiveness. Prisoners have served their punishment time, and the Lord will ultimately judge all of us. Let's leave the judgement to Him. The emphasis is upon repentance (turning your life around) and transformation. Christianity is about changed lives. It is not only the prisoner who is in the need of transformation. All of us who love the Lord are being gradually sanctified (or cleaned up). We should be responsive to our Lord, who created each of us. *God's desire is to reveal Himself and show compassion to those under the yoke of oppression - through us as instruments in His hands.* Come on, everyone! We are needed! This is the message I hope to share through this book. It is to the former prisoner and the homeless person that we turn our attention, considering Christian ministry and its positive influence in the process of rehabilitation, recovery, and rebuilding.

PREFACE

Why do we rely on the analysis of words, phrases, and sections of the Bible? I recognize the Bible as God's Word, an understanding shared by the vast majority of the Christian church. As such, we should be paying attention! Bible commentaries and handbooks describe the Bible as being written over a fifteen-hundred-year period by forty different writers. There are tens of thousands of manuscripts of the Old and New Testaments meticulously copied with amazing uniformity, more numerous than any other historical documents. Archaeological evidence of locations and artifacts from biblical history exist in many Middle Eastern areas and new discoveries are frequently being made.

The Bible makes claims about itself as being the Word of God:

> The prophet who has a dream, let him tell a
> dream; and he who has *My word*, let him speak
> *My word* faithfully. "What is the chaff to the
> wheat?" says the LORD. "Is not *My word* like

a fire?" says the LORD, "and like a hammer that breaks the rock in pieces? (Jeremiah 23:28-29).

The word of the LORD that came to Hosea (Hosea 1:1).

The word of the LORD that came to Joel (Joel 1:1). ...to whom *the word of God* came (and the Scripture cannot be broken)... (John 10:35).

All Scripture is given by inspiration of God, and is profitable for doctrine, for reproof, for correction, for instruction in righteousness (I Timothy 3:16).

Of this salvation the prophets have inquired and searched carefully, who prophesied of the grace that would come to you, searching what, or what manner of time, *the Spirit of Christ who was in them* was indicating when He testified beforehand the sufferings of Christ and the glories that would follow. To them it was revealed that, not to themselves, but to us they were ministering the things which now have been reported to you through those who have preached the gospel to you *by the Holy Spirit sent from heaven* - things which angels desire to look into (1 Peter 1:10-12).

And so we have the prophetic word confirmed, which you do well to heed as a light that shines in a dark place, until the day dawns and the morning star rises in your hearts; knowing this first, that no prophecy of Scripture is of any private interpretation, for prophecy never came by the will of man, but holy men of God spoke as they were moved *by the Holy Spirit* (2 Peter 1:19-21).

Those of us who accept the authorship of scripture as that of God Himself do so based upon faith, evidence and experience. Jesus tells a parable of the rich man and the beggar in Luke 16:19-31. In this parable, a rich man pleads with the patriarch Abraham to warn his five brothers about the torments of Hades. Abraham responds (in Jesus' telling of the parable): "If they do not hear Moses and the prophets, neither will they be persuaded though one rise from the dead" (Luke 16:31). Jesus did that very thing. He rose from the dead. This miracle of salvation has been well attested to. What about our brothers and sisters today? Should they be warned? The resurrected Jesus revealed Himself to the disciples near the end of the gospel of Luke: "Then He said to them, 'These are the words which I spoke to you while I was still with you, that all things must be fulfilled which were written in the Law of Moses and the Prophets and the Psalms concerning Me.' And He opened their understanding, that they might comprehend the Scriptures" (Luke 24:44-45). Lord, open our understanding today!

The Bible is not a book among holy books. It is exclusive, as is the Lord Himself. The American culture has come to believe that it doesn't matter what you believe. All faiths, in this lie of the devil, exemplify the same God. God is not a chameleon! God should be known and understood on God's terms!

CHAPTER 1

THE YOKE

Let me begin by providing the testimony of a person, the story of someone who was down but now is up with the help of God. My friend Richie was under the yoke of oppression, but has been saved, delivered, cleaned up, restored, transformed, and healed, resulting in his being an overcomer, bearing fruit, with joy, hope, blessing and fulfillment. He is redeemed through faith in Jesus Christ!

Richie told me once that he was the most wanted man in the city (by the police) a few years ago. He ran what he refers to as a drug house, himself using crack cocaine and heroin. He was surrounded by violence. People with addictions were shooting at each other. Richie remembers a few times he found himself picking up bullets from the kitchen floor. He was never shot, but his face was once beaten in very badly. This incident resulted in his being at the hospital that he was born in wondering whether he might also die there. He also has overdosed, three or four times, he can't remember which because of the fog he was living through. He was a prisoner for five years. But the saddest time in his life was when he was homeless. Richie describes that time as a low feeling, when he couldn't make his way to a friend's couch. His sons convinced him to get on the road to recovery through rehab. Henry Demers of Harmony Home, a Christian day-shelter in Manchester, New Hampshire, saw to it that Richie was sent by plane to California, where he spent six months at a Christian rehabilitation center known as Sovereign Health. Richie came back on fire for the Lord and determined to be an inspirational mentor to all of the people he encounters! It is more than two years since his return as of this writing, years of sobriety! He takes people to rehab, attends Alcoholics Anonymous and Narcotics Anonymous meetings, drives people to get their drivers licenses, and witnesses to everyone that the LORD saved his life and has transformed him. He told me his craving for drugs has been replaced with a craving for the Lord Himself. Richie has established his own painting business with his son Shayne who also has a testimony of recovery and victory in Jesus Christ. I spoke to him by phone recently and he described the beautiful sparkling water of Lake Sunapee next to a house he was painting. Rebuilding your life with God's help through faith in Jesus Christ is amazing! Richie mentions all the time: "It's awesome!" The yoke of oppression has been lifted off.

The visual metaphor of a yoke is a vivid one (a metaphor being a word or phrase which uses an object or action as a symbol or illustration to describe a concept). The yoke which weighs down beasts of burden and with a connected harness yanks then around, strongly illustrates the oppression of people being weighed down with a heavy load and led around where they may not want to go. We see this with so many who have been to prison, struggle with addiction, and/or find themselves homeless.

How does the Hebrew word, pronounced motah, or the Greek term, pronounced zygos, meaning "yoke" weave through Scripture? It is used sixty-one times in the Bible.

In Genesis 27:40, Isaac tells Esau, "you shall serve your brother; and it shall come to pass, when you become restless, that you shall *break his yoke* from your neck." Leviticus 26:13 reads, "I am the Lord your God, who brought you out of the land of Egypt, that you should not be their slaves; *I have broken the bands of your yoke* and made you walk upright." Wow. This is oppression – slavery oppression. Those mean Egyptian slave-drivers – do we have that kind of yoke in our midst? Deuteronomy 28:48 reads, "therefore you shall serve your enemies, whom the Lord will send against you, in hunger, in thirst, in nakedness, and in need of everything; and He will put a *yoke of iron* on your neck until He has destroyed you." Yikes. This is punishment "Because you [Israel] did not serve the Lord your God with joy and gladness of heart, for the abundance of everything" (Deuteronomy 28:47). The curses spoken of are a listing of those very needs that the Lord wants to see His people *have* as evidenced in the Isaiah 58 passage!

Let us listen in on Jeroboam and the whole congregation of Israel speaking to Rehoboam: "Your father *made our yoke heavy*; now therefore, lighten the burdensome service of your father, and his *heavy yoke* which he put on us, and we will serve you" (I Kings 12:4). This took place at the dividing of the kingdom! And the yoke spoken of here (twice in one verse) is indeed a political leadership heavily weighted *oppression*. There are multiple references to the concept of "yoke" as oppressive throughout I Kings and II Chronicles. Jeremiah 27 mentions "the *yoke of the king* of Babylon" three times and several times more throughout the book. It appears that we have tapped into a rich metaphoric vein. But this is not just a coincidence. There is a richness of meaning. In Lamentations 1:14 we see: "The *yoke of my transgressions* was bound; they were woven together by His hands, and thrust upon my neck. He made my strength fail; the Lord delivered me into the hands of those whom I am not able to withstand." This is pivotal – the yoke came from *my transgressions*. Does this mean I can exist in an atmosphere of oppression because of my own wrongdoing? Let us look to Jesus in order to remove the heaviness of this train of thought. In Matthew 11:29-30, Jesus says, "Take *My yoke* upon you and learn from Me, for I am gentle and lowly in heart, and you will find rest for your souls. For *My yoke is easy and My burden is light*." The vivid word-picture "yoke" does not suffer a transition in meaning between the Old and New Testaments.

Lamentations 1:14 speaks of "The yoke of my transgressions." It is easy to see that the yoke concept is connected to sin, or that we are under the yoke of sin. A yoke is described in many verses as referring to authorities, those in power. In some ways, we are like the children's story character Pinnochio, where the "yoke" of the marionette has strings, making us walk and act according to the will of the puppeteer. The devil, among other things, is a puppeteer. But the devil is not alone in pulling our individual strings. We wrestle against principalities and powers, "against the rulers of the darkness of this age, against spiritual hosts of wickedness in the heavenly places" (Ephesians 6:12). They in turn work through those in positions of power, who help to manipulate the yoke. When Jesus was arrested, He was arrested by chief priests, captains of the temple, and elders. And He spoke of "the power of darkness" (Luke 22:53). That power of darkness and the world system is at work today. It is a yoke. The chief priests, the captains of the temple, and the elders of today are susceptible to the tug of that yoke.

Consider the extended passage of Isaiah 58:6-9:

> Is this not the fast that I have chosen:
> To loose the bonds of wickedness,
> To undo the heavy burdens,
> To let the oppressed go free,
> And that you *break every yoke*?
> Is it not to share your bread with the hungry,
> And that you bring to your house the poor who
> are cast out;
> When you see the naked, that you cover him,
> And not hide yourself from your own flesh?
> Then your light shall break forth like the morning,
> Your healing shall spring forth speedily,
> And your righteousness shall go before you;

The glory of the LORD shall be your rear guard.
Then you shall call, and the LORD will answer;
You shall cry, and He will say, 'Here I am.'
"If you take away *the yoke from your midst*,
The pointing of the finger, and speaking
wickedness,

The presence of God is worth working toward. How should
we live in order to have the Lord respond, "Here I am," when
we pray to Him? It should be stated that the words of Isaiah in
this passage are intended for both the immediate audience and,
as prophecy, have meaning for all who would read it throughout time. "The address is indeed to Israel on earth, but we are
dull indeed if we cannot hear under it a word for ourselves."[10]
This passage indicates:

The LORD wants to be known.
The LORD reveals His desires to us.
The LORD is concerned about social justice.
We are being judged.
We have a role in helping the oppressed.
The LORD responds when we are obedient.
There is a yoke in our midst.

The passage, in a broad statement, can be understood as follows: "What kind of fast, what kind of sacrifice do I want from
you (says the LORD)? See to the needs of others, show mercy,
eliminate oppression, and then you will receive blessing!"

The LORD wants to be known. The Word of God is His revelation to us. The Bible is not the only way the LORD reveals Himself, but it is dependable and true. We should remember that the LORD has spoken in His Word, "let him who glories glory in this, *that he understands and knows Me*" (Jeremiah 9:24). How do we apply this understanding? *Seek the LORD.*

The LORD reveals His desires to us. In this passage, the Lord reveals what He wants. He explains what is better than a fast, what is more worthy than sacrifice. Do you want to give something up? Give up complacency! God is showing us what it means to Him when we do for others. What is our application? *Live your life according to the desires of the LORD.*

The LORD is concerned about social justice. Social justice, in its simplest form, is concern and help for those who are struggling. The *Oxford Reference Dictionary* defines *social justice* as: The objective of creating a fair and equal society in which each individual matters, their rights are recognized and protected, and decisions are made in ways that are fair and honest.[11] In Isaiah 3:15, the LORD says, "What do you mean by crushing My people and grinding the faces of the poor?" He calls the poor "My people." No distinction is being made whether they are of Israel. All people belong to the LORD. Jesus said "You shall love your neighbor as yourself" (Matthew 19:19), which is a repeat quote of Leviticus 19:18. There was a lawyer, a scribe who asked Jesus, "And who is my neighbor?" Then Jesus told the parable of the good Samaritan. His answer to "who is my neighbor?" was *the one who showed mercy.* So how do we respond? *Become concerned for the welfare of others.* The shorter answer is – *Show mercy.*

We are being judged. When our children are small, we watch them and we look out for them. As they approach adulthood, we are careful to know what they are up to, because we love them. We are the children of God, and He is paying attention to what we are doing. "The LORD looks down from heaven upon the children of men, to see if there are any who understand, who seek God" (Psalm 14:2). He wants to bless us! He has explained what He wants from us, and has promised to be there, to say, "Here I am," if only we will live our lives according to the desires of the LORD. How do we apply this understanding? *Live righteously before the LORD.*

We have a role in helping the oppressed. Christians are the hands and feet of Jesus until He returns. There is so much strife, so much oppression throughout the world. This Isaiah passage, as well as related texts, demonstrate that God desires our personal involvement in the realm of charity and help for the oppressed. There are often so many committee meetings and worship rehearsals and Bible studies in the life of a church, that there is not much time left for ministries which reach out to the needs of struggling people. Christians should be more deliberate about making opportunity for personal ministry. Individuals and groups of Christians should "break every yoke." New ministries can be established, and this is how the Kingdom of God gains a stronger foothold. Equally important is the benefit each person brings by coming alongside an existing ministry and providing support. Brothers and

sisters, we should – *Find a way to be in ministry where you are setting free the oppressed!*
The LORD responds when we are obedient. I have been to several countries of the mission field, on short-term trips, which were tremendously fulfilling. The presence of the LORD was at times quite powerful. How do you describe such things in words? I heard the LORD's voice on a mountaintop in Haiti. In Hong Kong and the Philippines, I was overwhelmed by the power of the presence of the Holy Spirit as I prayed for dozens of people, one at a time, and they slumped to the ground, crying and speaking in tongues, being blessed by the LORD in a major way right in front of me. My prayer was in undisrupted free flow despite my usually being tongue-tied and restrained, and I was hoarse from the emotion. There was a surge of power flowing through my shaking arms. I did my own slumping to the ground, seeing the tears of many others through my own tears from the awesome presence of the LORD, as I heard the words in my mind, "Here I Am, Here I Am, Here I Am!" The words of the book of Isaiah were coming true for me. Because of our efforts to reach out for the LORD and minister to the poor and oppressed, it felt like my righteousness was going before me. It felt like the glory of the Lord was my harvest, my rear guard. *Live in obedience to the Lord and expect great blessing!*

There is a yoke in our midst. This last thought seems to be anticlimactic; a downer after the announcement of the presence of the Lord; a check in contrast to the prior list of blessings. But it is front-page news among the dying newspapers, as well as the oldest story of all time. There was an accuser in that story; and hard work, tragedy, and despair resulted. Death became inevitable, and soon men began to oppress. The yoke is representative of a fallen world. There is a contemporary way to express part of what it means to "take away the yoke from your midst" – *Don't be part of the problem*. Identify any traces of a yoke in your own behavior and be aware, be sensitive to ways in which others are being downtrodden. Fight it! Tear it apart! Go against the tide and against the yoke! Be a resource, an instrument for the light and healing and glory of the Lord. Break the mold of the yoke of oppression – Live for the LORD, respond to Him, and tell Him, as Isaiah did when the LORD asked, "who will go for Us? Isaiah had the boldness to respond, "Here am I, send me" (Isaiah 6:8). The best way to fast for the LORD, to offer your sacrifice, is to offer your very self. If you long to hear Him say, "Here I am" when you pray, you should first say, "Here *I* am" to serve and to break every yoke.

CHAPTER 2

TO BE A CHRISTIAN IS TO HAVE A MISSION

Our Father has always longed to be in fellowship with us. The LORD God called out so long ago to Adam (whose name means "man") in the garden: "Where are you?" (Genesis 3:9). He continues to ask us today: "Man, woman, where are you?" Our lives are more fulfilling when we live them out in co-operation with God, who made all of us in the first place. To know and love God is to have a greater sense of having a mission in life.

My friend Sister Liza lives with an understanding that her purpose and mission is in serving God. I know her as a sup-porter and volunteer with 1269 Café outreach to the homeless. She has been criticized for praying on the steps of her children's high school and she has advocated for the homeless with vigils at the state capital building. What I find staggering is her continued concern and ongoing advocating for the housing needs of sex offenders. Here is just a short testimony from her sent by phone text:

> I am a survivor of sexual assault. My trauma and PTSD [Post Traumatic Stress Disorder] has been life long beginning in early childhood at just 8 years of age. Our Lord and Savior, Jesus Christ, is the only hope there is for victims to truly be healed, be taught to forgive, and not dwell on negative feelings.
>
> The love of Jesus is the purest brightest light in the darkness of sexual violence trauma and all mental turbulence and distress caused by being a victim of a crime, He is salvation and shelter from evil.
>
> The most gracious and merciful, God Almighty, has called me to work in His ministry and share His mercy, grace, and teach others of salvation. Repentance from sin is the only way to God's promises, paradise and eternal life.

Sister Liza's capacity for forgiveness is astounding. She has turned her victimization around and made it a cause, a mission to help others in need. She understands where her strength to overcome has come from, and she wants people who struggle to know and experience that source of strength.

Our LORD Jesus Christ announced Himself as Messiah and described His mission when He read the messianic description out of the book of the prophet Isaiah at the synagogue in Nazareth:

> The Spirit of the LORD is upon Me,
> Because He has anointed Me
> To preach the gospel to the poor;
> He has sent Me to heal the brokenhearted,
> To proclaim liberty to the captives
> And recovery of sight to the blind,
> To set at liberty those who are oppressed;
> To proclaim the acceptable year of the LORD.
> Luke 4:18-19

This declaration was written by the Holy Spirit through the prophet Isaiah seven hundred years prior. It is indeed the mission of Jesus Christ. *His mission is our mission!* To be a Christian is to have a mission! What is our mission? We are to preach the gospel to the poor; heal the brokenhearted; proclaim liberty to the captives; help the blind recover their sight; and set at liberty those who are oppressed![12]

A significant parallel to the Isaiah 58 passage is seen just three chapters further on in Isaiah 61. Jesus read Isaiah 61:1-2a in the synagogue (Luke 4:18-19), and indicated that this specific Scripture was fulfilled in Him. In other words, He was (and is) the Messiah written about by Isaiah. Let us consider that passage and some close parallels from Isaiah 58:6-9:

preach good tidings to the poor	bring to your house the poor
heal the brokenhearted	your healing shall spring forth
proclaim liberty to the captives	let the oppressed go free
opening of the prison to those who are bound	loose the bonds of wickedness
EXCERPTS FROM ISAIAH 61: 1	EXCERPTS FROM ISAIAH 58: 6-9

What are the common themes in both passages? *The poor, healing, setting free, the oppressed, those in bondage* are seen in both sections of Scripture. In chapter 58, "the oppressed" literally means "the ones crushed." Our LORD is undoubtedly concerned about the poor and the oppressed. Concern for the oppressed poor is also evident in Isaiah 3:15: "What do you mean by crushing My people and grinding the faces of the poor?" Both aspects of crushing and grinding are attributed to those oppressed. Psalm12:5 reads, " 'For the oppression of the poor, for the sighing of the needy, now I will arise,' says the LORD; 'I will set him in the safety for which he yearns.' "

In Nehemiah 5:10-12, we see an example of *loosening the bonds of wickedness*. Nehemiah pleads, "Please, let us stop this usery!" In Jeremiah 34:9, we see *letting the oppressed go free*, "every man should set free his male and female slave – a Hebrew man or woman – that no one should keep a Jewish brother in bondage."

In Ezekiel, we see the following words of the LORD:

> But if a man is just and does what is lawful and
> right;...
> *If he has not oppressed anyone,...*

But has given his bread to the hungry and covered
the naked with clothing;
If he has not exacted usery...
If he has walked in My statutes And kept My
judgments faithfully –
He is just; He shall surely live!' Says the LORD
GOD (Ezekiel 18:5,7-9).

These sentiments mirror the wisdom of Isaiah 58:6-9.

Consider the words of Jesus: "For I was hungry and you gave Me food; I was thirsty and you gave Me drink; I was a stranger and you took Me in; I was naked and you clothed Me; I was sick and you visited Me; I was in prison and you came to Me" (Matthew 25:35-36). These actions of compassion are examples of the will of the LORD for our lives. James 2:15-16 points out, "If a brother or sister is naked and destitute of daily food, and one of you says to them, 'Depart in peace, be warmed and filled,' but you do not give them the things which are needed for the body, what does it profit?" Compassion, justice, mercy – these are the desires of the LORD.

In Hosea 6: 6, the LORD says, "I desire mercy and not sacrifice." Jesus quotes this very passage twice, in Matthew 9:13 and 12:7. Fasting is the kind of sacrifice which the LORD sees as inferior to mercy. In I Samuel 15:22, we see a similar verse: "Has the LORD as great delight in burnt offerings and sacrifices, as in obeying the voice of the LORD? Behold, to obey is better than sacrifice."[13] Obeying the voice of the LORD in behaving mercifully to other people is better than making a sacrifice. Jesus reaffirms this in Matthew 5:23-24, "Therefore if you bring your gift to the altar, and there remember that your brother has something against you, leave your gift there before the altar, and go your way. First be reconciled to your brother, and then come and offer your gift." The prophet Micah provides this insight: "He has shown you, O man, what is good; and what does the LORD require of you but *to do justly, to love mercy*, and to walk humbly with your God?" (Micah 6:8).

In verse 9 of Isaiah 58, there is a description of what happens "then" when you follow the "if" of the prior verses. "Then you shall call, and the LORD will answer, you shall cry out, and He will say, Here I am." In contrast Micah 3:4 makes the point of judgement upon those who "hate good and love evil" (Micah 3:2). "Then they will cry to the LORD, but He will not hear them; He will even hide His face from them at that time, because they have been evil in their deeds." Micah 3:4 speaks of judgment, while Isaiah 58:9 speaks of blessing. But the unifying concept is *obedience to the will of the LORD.*[14]

In Isaiah 58:9 we have the very presence of God. "Here I am," He states. This presence is what people all over the world yearn for. In *Joy Unspeakable*, Martin-Lloyd Jones recounts the experiences of several men (from their writings) of the overwhelming presence of God. He names John Owen (a Puritan), Thomas Goodwin (of Oxford), John Wesley, Jonathan Edwards, D.L. Moody, George Whitefield, and Edward Elton. The quotations from these men are extensive, and an exemplary phrase from D.L. Moody shall provide a sense of these experiences: "I can only say, God revealed Himself to me, and

I had such an experience of His love that I had to ask Him to stay His hand."[15] Whitefield characterizes a frequent response to the presence of God as follows: "My own soul was so full that I retired and wept before the LORD, and had a deep sense of my own vileness, and the sovereignty and greatness of God's everlasting Love."

J.I. Packer writes that we are made to know God.[16] The LORD wants to be known. "For I desire mercy and not sacrifice, and the knowledge of God more than burnt offerings" (Hosea 6:6). The knowledge of God is more important than sacrifice; more important than fasting. God wants to be known.

> Thus says the LORD: Let not the wise man glory in his wisdom, let not the mighty man glory in his might, nor let the rich man glory in his riches; but let him who glories glory in this, *that he understands and knows Me, that I am the LORD, exercising lovingkindness, judgment, and righteousness in the earth*, for these I delight, says the LORD (Jeremiah 9:23-24).

How does the LORD exercise lovingkindness, judgement, and righteousness in the earth? *He needs His followers to cooperate.* Our very lives are lived out in either cooperation or noncooperation with the will of God, and the tendency is toward the 'non.' In the exercising of lovingkindness there is loosening of the bonds of wickedness, undoing of the cords of the yoke, setting free the oppressed, sharing food with the hungry, tending to the homeless poor, and clothing the naked. It has been mentioned that salvation and justice must coexist, and justice does not exist in a vacuum. *We must act.*

The LORD is concerned for social justice. There are many secular people concerned for this same cause, and the motivation springs from a humanitarian impulse (which of course is God-given). And there are secular organizations doing great work in the areas of sharing food, providing shelter and clothing – often in greater measure than Christian groups or organizations. Is social justice a side-trip, a distraction, or should it be central to the Christian experience? My answer (in part) to this question is: "What would you do in order to witness the presence of God?" Isaiah 58:6-9 makes a strong case for social justice – for concern for the poor, homeless, wretched, and oppressed. Consider the revelation of Jesus Christ to the church at Laodicea (a city like many cities of today): "Because you say, 'I am rich, have become wealthy, and have need of nothing' – and do not know that you are wretched, miserable, poor, blind, and naked" (Revelation 3:17). The people you help are an extension of yourself. You may be comfortable in your nice home. Praise God for that! Within miles of where you live people are in deep need of help.

Jesus told us that when you do this "to one of the least of these," that you do this for Him (Matthew 25:45). Jesus' mission to us is to preach the gospel to the poor; to heal the brokenhearted; to preach deliverance to the captives; to set at liberty those who are oppressed," and the LORD compels us to loose the bonds of wickedness; set free the oppressed; share your bread with the hungry, bring in the homeless; clothe the naked" These are descriptions of *how you do social justice.* The LORD is concerned about social justice *and so should we.* This is the mission of the Christian.

CHAPTER 3

LOVINGKINDNESS IN ACTION

Several years ago, I was doing evangelism as part of a mission team called Fishers of Men Medical Ministries. We were on a trip to Ghana, Africa. Medical clinics were held in a stationary small hospital and mobile teams went to different regions. I was struck by the similarity of the people and conditions of Ghana in comparison to the many times I had been to the Caribbean island nation of Haiti. In both locations, women carried loads on their heads, men held machetes almost as an extension of their arms, farmers burned brush in the fields, and thatch roofs were built with identical technique. Then it dawned me – the people of both countries are blood relatives of each other. They have been forcibly separated from each other because of the slave trade, with more than two-hundred and fifty years of generations living apart. The Lord was showing me a broken family. On some level, every person can identify with a broken family.

While in Ghana, we took an opportunity to visit one of the slave castles or fortresses along the southern coastline. The Elmina slave castle or dungeon is a whitewashed stone and mortar structure with high walls. It is stark and formidable. Tour guides provided the history of the slave trade throughout western Africa. Several castles dot the Gulf of Guinea in the tropical region of the Atlantic Ocean. They served as holding cells, dungeons of suffering and deprivation. The Elmina slave castle has an inner courtyard, adjacent administrative rooms, with tunnels, individual cells, and large dark dungeons below. The infamous "door of no return" is located on an outside wall, facing the ocean.

I took the photograph above, which is shown in a tiny size because there isn't much to see. There was very little light inside and the resulting daylight outside was bright by contrast. There are two boats in the distance on the water. People who had been abducted as slaves, after being herded into a dungeon under inhumane, unsanitary conditions – were lowered down by a ramp into small boats and brought out to ships where they were shoved below decks as cargo. After being pushed through that doorway, they were never to see their homeland again.

As part of the tour of Elmira castle, a group of about twenty-five visitors, including me, were briefed about the Dutch and British part in the slave trade as we stood together in one of the large dungeons. Men and women captive slaves were held there separately. They were shackled and packed together so tightly, they couldn't lie down. They were given very little food or water. There was no "going to the bathroom." They relieved themselves in place. There was illness and death (before they were packed into ships, where there was more illness and death). I recall looking up at a tiny window in the stone wall that provided inadequate ventilation. *And then the team of two tour guides closed the iron grate door, locked it, and walked away.* We visitors understood that the tour guides wanted to give us a tiny glimpse of being closed in, incarcerated, under oppression, in bondage. There was some nervous laughter. They returned after only five minutes. It was a pretty good object lesson, and the overall impact of touring this castle/fortress/dungeon was to have heightened sympathy and compassion for those who are oppressed.

Cruelty and oppression are not exclusive to the 1700's or any other era. Today's halfway house residents and homeless people have not been made slaves, yet many have suffered abuse; many have been enslaved by an addiction. The poor and needy may have been victimized, may have made poor life choices. It's not our place to judge people who struggle. "Judge not that you be not judged" (Matthew 7:1). We are called to demonstrate lovingkindness.

The first three verses of chapter 13 of the Book of Hebrews in the New Testament speak of brotherly love, caring for strangers, prisoners, and those that are mistreated. They exhibit a pattern seen throughout Scripture. The overwhelming impression made by these verses is one of compassion. The LORD is exhorting us to treat others compassionately. So much of Hebrews involves what we should believe, yet in these verses we are told what we should *do*. Being involved in compassionate ministry is where the action is in Christianity, where Christianity comes alive.

> *"Let brotherly love continue. Do not forget to entertain strangers, for by so doing some have unwittingly entertained angels. Remember the prisoners as if chained with them—those who are mistreated—since you yourselves are in the body also."*
> (Hebrews 13:1-3)[17]

Isaiah 61:1 resonates with Hebrews 13:1-3 in exemplary harmony when it mentions "He has sent Me to heal the brokenhearted, to proclaim liberty to the captives, and the opening of the prison to those who are bound..." There is also a strong similarity seen in Isaiah 58:6-9. Let us consider some of these similarities:

Let brotherly love continue	
preach good tidings to the poor	bring to your house the poor
Entertain strangers	
heal the brokenhearted	your healing shall spring forth
Remember the prisoners as if chained with them	
proclaim liberty to the captives	let the oppressed go free
those who are mistreated	
opening of the prison to those who are bound	loose the bonds of wickedness
EXCERPTS FROM HEBREWS 13:1-3	
EXCERPTS FROM ISAIAH 61: 1	EXCERPTS FROM ISAIAH 58: 6-9

Patterns of similarity between the Hebrew Old Testament and the Greek New Testament reveal the handiwork, indeed, the lovingkindness of the LORD. Bringing "to your house the poor" is certainly a way of showing "hospitality to strangers." There is overlapping symbolism in the terms: "captives" and "prisoners;" "chained" and "those who are bound;" and the "mistreated" and "oppressed." The pattern revealed in this set of scripture verses is overwhelmingly compassionate. These passages indicate the motivation that our LORD Jesus exemplified, and provides for us our "marching orders" for Christian ministry.[18]

What are the Characteristics of those who God
wants to unbind?

poor/ brokenhearted/ in need of healing/ captive/
in need of deliverance/ those who are mistreated/
in need of liberty/ oppressed/ in need of recovery

This book is written out of concern for those that are
homeless and those in halfway houses that have been in prison. Let us consider what God is saying in verse Hebrews 13:3,
"Remember the prisoners as if chained with them-- those who
are mistreated-- since you yourselves are in the body also."[19]
This single verse demonstrates the lovingkindness, mercy, and
compassion of God. This exhortation moves past the stranger previously mentioned, the one whose character you do not
know – to a known criminal, yet the LORD commends us to
remember the prisoner (as in visit; treat with kindness; comfort). In short, the LORD wants us to extend His lovingkindness. We should share through our concern the chains or fetters
of the one being punished. Jesus puts Himself in the place of
whichever prisoner we are willing to visit, when He says, "I was
in prison and you came to Me" (Matthew 25:36). Prisoners
are mentioned in Hebrews 10:34 and 11:36. In both instances
these are Christians being persecuted for their faith. "There but
for the Grace of God go I," whether through persecution, or by
transgression. The LORD is exhorting us to visit and comfort
the prisoner in any event. "Those who are mistreated" bring to
mind "those who are oppressed," which we have seen in Isaiah.
The "mistreated" include prisoners and others who suffer.

"Since you yourselves are in the body also" has a range of possible meanings.

- Option A: You have the weakness of carnal flesh. You have temptations and you give into them. Who are you to turn your nose up at the prisoner, a fellow sinner?
- Option B: You are connected in a church fellowship, which is supposed to demonstrate the mercy of God. Take mercy upon the prisoner because you are part of the body of Christ.
- Option C (according to David DeSilva): Remember the prisoner, *as if you were in their skin.*[20]

We are to have compassion for the prisoner and the mistreated. The LORD has compassion for prisoners; and if we are to mimic Him, so should we. The LORD Himself was made *incarnate*, a term which literally means 'came into the skin of:' "And the Word became flesh and dwelt among us" (John 1:14). If we are to love our neighbor (Matthew 19:19), we are to "get into the skin of" those who struggle. The modern equivalent colloquialism would be "walk a mile in their shoes."[21] *The Geneva Study Bible* paraphrases this verse: "Be so touched, as if their misery were yours."[22]

A Greek term is seen in Hebrews 13:3, from the phrase "Remember the prisoners as if chained with them." The term is tremendously significant, and speaks to an underlying motivation for Christian missions and ministry. Pronounced "sundedemenoy." it literally means to be bound together with, be in prison with.[23,] The equivalent Hebrew term, as seen in Isaiah

61:1 in the phrase "the opening of the prison to those who are *bound*" is pronounced "welissareem," meaning *fetter, imprisoned, tie up, harness, yoke, bind oneself to a vow.*[24] This is part of the passage which Jesus reads in Luke 4:18, *as He is describing what He has been anointed to do.* The term *sundedemenov* is unique (a single application of the passive voice). Its meaning goes beyond "bound." *It literally means "to be bound together with." The term "yoke" is included as part of the definition.*

We are prisoners when we are bound to sin. But the LORD's mission, together with all of us who want to love and serve Him, is to "Remember the prisoners as if chained with them," and work toward "the opening of the prison to those who are *bound*." Amazingly, in the process of freeing the prisoner yoked to sin and oppression, Jesus Himself died a prisoner.

Hebrews 13:3 helps to establish motivation for sympathetic concern and engaging in help for those who have struggled through being "bound" and incarcerated. The contemporary halfway house for former prisoners is an extension of that very circumstance. Indeed, the halfway house is the intersection between freedom and home, a midpoint rife with peril, a time of deep need. When you minister to others in times of deep need, you are an extension of God's lovingkindness.[25]

CHAPTER 4

PRISONER REHABILITATION

It is important to understand prison life and the challenges of readjustment if you are to come alongside and administer aid during the time of readjustment. Halfway houses are the interconnection between prison and home, providing housing for the vulnerable former prisoner making his or her way back into the world. It is clear that rehabilitation should begin in prison and should be an intentional process throughout the time spent there. *Rehabilitation* is training, education, counseling and mentoring of inmates with an eye toward preparing the released former prisoner to be a contributor to society, and for the sake of public safety. Frequently not enough rehabilitation takes place in prison, and help is needed during the readjustment time after release from prison.

The Christian walk in life, being in fellowship with our LORD God through faith in Jesus Christ, is the best form of rehabilitation, the best means of recovery, the best way to rebuild your life on planet Earth. There are many rehabilitation methods and Twelve-Step programs, and when you add a Christian love for God to any method or program, your chance for success rises dramatically. The previous statements are totally biased, but they are based upon trust and confidence. Faith itself is based upon trust and confidence. The statements are also based upon experience – twenty years of personal conversations with prisoners and former prisoners, and the testimonies spoken by them.

Jesus said, "The thief does not come except to steal, and to kill, and to destroy. I have come that they may have life, and that they may have it more abundantly!" (John 10:10). Our LORD desires abundant life for us, and the heart of the follower of Jesus should extend to those former inmates in need of more abundant lives. Not every church has mature members who accept former inmates into their fellowship. When a church is known for helping those who struggle with reentry however, there is support, encouragement, and accountability beyond that of a coach or mentor. A good church is a network of support – someone who may know of a job, someone who knows where an apartment can be rented, someone who has a truck to help carry furniture. A good church also encourages faith and a relationship with God through prayer, worship, and continual reminders of the God's wisdom of God through His Word. I know of many success stories, men and women who have rebuilt careers, reconnected and established families, and have homes surrounded by loved ones. Most of these men and women are dedicated to following the LORD.

When we consider rehabilitation, it is done so with a vision of future freedom. *Rehabilitation* is vital for the success of that future state of freedom, it is the term used for *what society wants to happen to the prisoner.* The concept is looking from the outside in. From the standpoint of the prisoner subjected to having done time in prison, I believe the better concept, the better viewpoint, is the idea of rebuilding. Rebuilding is a cause we can all get behind. I tell folks all of the time, "See yourself as an overcomer rebuilding your life."

Lennie Spitale, the author of *Prison Ministry*, has been a guest speaker throughout New England and has served in ministry at the New Hampshire State Prison for Men in Concord. He and I have met and we each have been guest speakers at the annual Christian Aftercare Ministries banquets. Some of the men of the Calumet Halfway House that this writer has met through a Transformational Life Coaching ministry have known him. Spitale's insights on prison ministry carry over into the environment of the halfway house. Spitale writes of issues of self-esteem and identity: "Most of the guys I know resent the word *institutionalization,* or its sister phrase, *becoming institutionalized.* And, I think, rightly so. By its very nature, it is a dehumanizing word. Prisoners view it as lumping everyone into a category of characteristics that, while perhaps of interest to sociologists, tend to erase their own uniqueness and individuality."[26] Life coaching with the men at the halfway house and at Helping Hands Outreach has been an opportunity to support and draw out their uniqueness and individuality and help them to have a fighting chance at rebuilding their lives.

In their book *Beyond Bars: Rejoining Society after Prison,* Jeffrey Ian Ross and Stephen C. Richards refer to "the criminal justice system as a 'perpetual incarceration machine' " that "continues to grow because of its failure to reform or rehabilitate inmates."[27] They paint a bleak outlook: "Prison has a strange way of converting relatively mild-mannered, peaceful men and women into desperados who would rather shoot it out with law enforcement than return to the penitentiary. They turn 'outlaw'; because they know they 'can't make it' on the outside and they no longer care what happens to them or anyone else in the community." These statements are a generalization, and it is imprecise to profile any group of people, but sadly, there are many individuals who fit the description.

Ross and Richards are concerned for the dysfunctional correctional system that exists and grows: "The sad part is that the criminal justice machinery depends upon a growing inmate population to guarantee continued funding and employment for correctional facilities and their staff... The U. S. government has built mega correctional complexes all over the country."[28] It certainly does not appear that a "correctional" process is succeeding. It is vital for people to come alongside and help individuals who have been subjected to our current "criminal justice machinery."

The historical use of prisons has been to punish and shut away the offender. "For too long American criminologists, legislators, and judges have operated on the premise that the law is the primary means of crime control… It is unreasonable to expect such a system to make material changes in a society and its culture."[29] Lois G. Forer goes on to say, "What is needed is a new philosophy, one that is based on public safety rather than the punishment of sinners." Robert Johnson also weighs in with an historical perspective: "The challenge, then, is to break this destructive cycle and to begin instead to build the bonds that sustain the social body. Debts must be paid, to be sure, but so too must new lives commence. Historically, the prison has failed at this task; it has too often been neither civilized nor civilizing."[30]

Many attest to the need for a rehabilitation process during the extended years of incarceration. The rehabilitation process stands against the motivation of punishment, payment for crime, and institutionalization. Robert Johnson states that "all prisoners should both be supported in their prison adjustment efforts and offered the opportunity to acquire the social, educational, and vocational skills needed to live a peaceful and ultimately self-sufficient life upon release from confinement." Johnson believes that intentional rehabilitation aids in the process of reintegration into the community, the very point at which they are residents of halfway houses: "…the experience of reintegration into the free community must be an ongoing process rather than an event reserved for those inmates who are about to be released."

Karl Menninger addresses a root motive for the punishment for crime: "Personal revenge we have renounced, but official legalized revenge we can still enjoy... a hurt to society should be repaid."[31] This view, which emphasizes the punishment side of the spectrum, as opposed to rebuilding or rehabilitation, makes no provision for the life to still be lived. And the life still to be lived involves loved ones, extended family, and society in general. Helping the offender helps all those connected.

Francis Allen emphasizes the importance of *transformation* when he writes, "The British philosopher Jeremy Bentham wrote in *The Theory of Legislation*: "It is a great merit in a punishment to contribute to the reformation of the offender, not only through fear of being punished again, but by a change in his character and habits."[32]

Victoria R. DeRosia writes of "the shift in punishment philosophies from rehabilitation to retribution and incapacitation."[33] She asks, "How much of the disorder in the nation's prisons is attributable to management problems related to institutional security, methods of control, and the custodians themselves?" These aspects of punishment, payment for crime, and institutionalization represent the backdrop of experience the resident of the halfway house continues to live with. A few coaching sessions or a teaching program cannot completely rehabilitate a former inmate. But a few coaching sessions or a teaching program can at least provide a fighting chance for the client to pursue a path of healing.

Richard Bovan is an ex-prisoner and author who titles his introduction as "Change, Change, Change is What It's All About."[34] He outlines *10 Rules for Making it in Society After Doing Time: The Dedicated Ex-Prisoner's Guide to Life and Success on the Outside.* Rule number five has an emphasis pertinent to the coaching process: "Envision your path to success; have a realistic plan." This is exactly where coaching dovetails into the needs of the former inmate.

Demico Booth is another ex-prisoner and author who repeats a statement mentioned by Richard Bovan: "Proper Preparation Prevents Poor Performance."[35] He refers to this motto as the "Five P's of Success," and mentions his own "Three P's." – Proper Prison Planning, stating in all caps, "PLANNING IS AN INTEGRAL PART OF SUCCESS."[36] Booth expounds on the importance of planning during a person's prison time. This would certainly help when a person reaches a halfway house, if that's where they have been sent. Bovan and Booth each also advocate for the process of visioning and setting goals.

Former President Jimmy Carter lends his voice in support of the need for Christian prison ministry, as a ninety-three year old: "I believe now, more than ever, that Christians are called to plunge into the life of the world, and to inject the moral and ethical values of our faith into the process of governing."[37] President Carter includes a portion of a speech that he made to "fellow Baptists in 1978," [italicized in his book]:

What are the goals of a person or a denomination or a country? They are all remarkably the same: a desire for peace; a need for humility, for examining one's faults and turning away from them; a commitment to human rights in the broadest sense of the words, based on a moral society concerned with the alleviation of suffering because of deprivation or hatred or hunger or physical affliction; and a willingness, even an eagerness, to share one's ideals, one's faith with others, to translate love in a person to justice.

President Carter brought his Christian faith to the White House and back home again. He states, "More recently, since our years in the White House, I have tended to move away from politics and toward religion, but the two are still related." Just as the researcher Byron R. Johnson advocates "partnerships between sacred and secular" on behalf of those who struggle, President Carter shares this point of view.

The gospel of John records Jesus' arrest: "Then the detachment of troops and the captain and the officers of the Jews arrested Jesus and bound Him" (John 18:12). From the time of Jesus' arrest, and throughout His interrogation, trials, and death, *Jesus was a prisoner.* Jesus died a prisoner. Those who embrace faith in Jesus Christ as LORD and Savior are connecting with One who understands isolation, punishment, abuse, hardship, pain, and brutality. He suffered to the point of death.

To lean on the LORD Jesus is to lean upon Someone who understands your pain and trials, if you are or if you have been imprisoned. The hope is to communicate this reality to former prisoners as we minister to them.

CHAPTER 5

REENTRY

Rehabilitation and reentry back to life in the general public is part of a continuum for the prisoner or former prisoner. To put it mildly, a tough burden falls on the reentry process. At the point of release into a halfway house, former inmates are expected to reintegrate, find work. establish a home, and reconnect with family, but they are frequently ill-equipped to do so.

Chuck Colson is famous for establishing the international ministry to prisoners known as Prison Fellowship. In his book, *My Final Word: Holding Tight to the Issues that Matter Most,* Colson describes the prisoner in a unique way: "One of the great distinctives about the ministry of Prison Fellowship is that we are targeted toward not only the poor, who obviously have a special place in God's heart, but the poorest of the poor: the prisoner. He's helpless, powerless, has no resources, no freedom. He has been stripped of everything, which, when you come right down to it, is the best definition of *poor.*"[38] As he continues to describe *the poorest of the poor,* Colson provides an image of the former prisoner who is newly released:

> You have to really understand what being poor is. It doesn't just mean you're living below the poverty level or that you are hungry for your next meal. It means that you are absolutely powerless. You have no human resources. You have just been released from prison. You have twenty-five or a hundred dollars, a bus ticket home, an old suit of clothes, and there you are, no friends, no place you can go. Nobody will take you in; nobody wants you. Where do you turn?

Chuck Colson's description of the released prisoner is quite poignant, and nearly identical to the experience of the men who arrive at the Calumet Halfway House. They do have the house, however. The image of a lone person on the side of the street with a need to go somewhere – becomes a motivation to extend ministry, to provide a helping hand.

Kent R. Kerley writes, "I spent the last decade [as of 2014] going into prisons and halfway houses to study people who have committed all sorts of horrific crimes, mostly while under the influence of hard-core drugs – but now claim to be 'changed,' 'saved,' or 'born again.' The underlying reason they cited for their dramatic change was a new or renewed religious faith."[39] Kerley goes on to ask these questions: "How does religious faith in prisons and halfway houses help offenders of all types to cope with the difficult institutional environment? What tools does faith provide for life after release from prisons and halfway houses?"

Is there a basis, beyond that of faith, for having confidence in the effectiveness of bible studies and Christian mentoring programs in both the prison setting and in halfway houses? Kerley, "an independent researcher," is the author of *Religious Faith in Correctional Contexts.* He states, "My collaborators and I simply analyze the data and report the results."[40] Kerley's book is a study of studies (his second chapter includes more than thirty other studies). Does Kerley support faith-based programs? He writes:

> I support any correctional treatment program with these characteristics:
>
> (1) it has at least modest empirical support (quantitative and qualitative) based on scholarly research, (2) it does not jeopardize the safety and welfare of inmates or correctional staff, (3) it is not coercive, illegal, or unethical, (4) it gives inmates something constructive to do with their time, and (5) its cost is not prohibitive for state or federal governments.
>
> *It seems clear to me that faith-based programs in prisons and in halfway houses typically have high scores on all five of these criteria* [italics added].

This is a sound endorsement by a dedicated researcher. Byron R. Johnson has written *More God, Less Crime: Why Faith Matters and How It Could Help More* (2011). He reviewed 272 studies from between 1944 and 2010. This is simply an astounding level of investigation! Johnson found that in 90 percent of these studies, the authors reported an "inverse or beneficial relationship between religion and some measure of crime or delinquency."[41]

Johnson points out a hurdle for communities of faith: "In an age of political correctness, perhaps the last acceptable prejudice is the one leveled against the involvement of highly religious people and their faith-based approaches to social problems – problems the government cannot fix without them." There is indeed a bias, a stigma against the faith community, born of the assumption that spiritual matters have no scientific basis, that faith and science are opposites. Johnson states, "Without faith-based or community organizations serving as intermediaries to bridge the gap between disadvantaged populations and the resources they need, high-risk groups will likely remain beyond effective reach and service."

Johnson addresses the increasing need for accommodating former prisoners with some staggering numbers:

> As long as prisons have existed, ex-prisoners have had difficulty in transitioning back to society. What is different today is the sheer magnitude of prisoners leaving prisons and returning to American communities each year. In less

than three decades, the U. S. prison population has increased 482 percent. Approximately two thousand prisoners are being released from prisons each day, a trend that is expected to continue into the foreseeable future.

Johnson is adamant that "correctional initiatives" must continue: "Halfway houses, community corrections programs, intensive supervision, and community reintegration programs represent but a few of the various post-release efforts designed to make the transition back to society less difficult for ex-prisoners." Johnson is an advocate of the role of halfway houses, yet acknowledges that the struggle is difficult. Reentry has dismal prospects, indeed. It is a dire circumstance. Johnson writes: "concern is growing that the increasing numbers of ex-prisoners returning to communities all across the country will become a major threat to public safety. In a Department of Justice – sponsored report, leading experts agree that the successful reintegration of former prisoners is one of the most formidable challenges facing society today." Christian ministry seeks to address this "formidable challenge."

In its additional introductory material, *The Prison Bible* makes this poignant observation: "Most inmates find it hard to understand the process it takes to become a different person on the outside of prison. Many of them think their freedom from prison means they are now free from all restrictions. They will not submit to rules or any authority after they are released, including God's."[42] This is truly a valuable insight. Any who wish to minister to former inmates should bear this in mind as one of the challenges of reentry.

Among the challenges of reintegration is the following stark truth: "Everyone must pull his own weight."[43] For Robert P. Lupton, author of *Compassion, Justice, and the Christian Life: Rethinking Ministry to the Poor,*" pulling your own weight "is the key to responsible charity – which is not to say that everyone has equal capacity – just equal responsibility. When individuals, like communities, assume responsibility for their own destiny, when they abandon self-pity, self-indulgence and blame to face the hard work of building (or rebuilding) their lives, they have taken a giant step toward health."

Despite the challenges of reintegration, Louis B. Cei writes of the potential value of faith-based initiatives: "a 2002 meta-analysis by the University of Pennsylvania reviewed 46 studies of religious programs and concluded that "research on religious practices... indicates that higher levels of religious involvement are associated with... lower rates of delinquency among youth and reduced criminal activity among adults."[44]

Seiter and Kadela (2003) identified effective reentry services and programs:

> vocational training and work release programs were effective for reducing recidivism and improving job readiness skills; drug treatment was effective for reducing drug use, recidivism, drug-related crimes, and parole violations; educational programs increased educational

achievement scores but did not decrease recidivism; halfway house programs reduced severe criminal behavior; and prerelease programs reduced recidivism.[45]

Halfway house programs were found to reduce severe criminal behavior. The environment of a halfway house is not as restrictive as a prison, but there is dormitory-style housing, or at least shared housing by a large group of all men or all women. There are rules to follow, and expectations for the resident to be seeking work or out working. Also, there are probation officers who make demands for counseling, Alcoholics Anonymous or Narcotics Anonymous meetings, or drug rehab programs depending on the needs of the particular resident. It stands to reason that if a former inmate wants a new start, a halfway house *which helps him or her to access resources*, provides then a fighting chance.

Laurie C. Bright and Mary G. Graham write, "faith-based programs – both prison-based and community-based – can provide much needed services. Government agencies, given their structure and specific missions, can find it difficult to match some of these services."[46] This is especially true due to the number of volunteers in these programs. Bright and Graham go on to mention, "faith-based groups provide assistance that draws upon and reflects community values and culture. Their position within the community offers ties that are perhaps most important for giving offenders a better chance for success when they return home." One of the benefits of the

Calumet Halfway House and Helping Hands Outreach being on the same street, is the availability of several churches in the immediate area. There are some which specifically understand and cater to those who are former prisoners.

Harold Dean Trulear writes of the benefits of a church network for those who have been former inmates, "Congregations represent a rich resource for assisting men and women returning from incarceration (returning citizens) in their reintegration to society. While recent efforts in the public and private sector have focused on the provision of services such as employment, housing, mentoring and substance abuse, research indicates that support systems that provide pro-social life skills are an important part of the reentry process."[47]

Jeananne Markway and Doug Worsham are also supportive of faith-based contributions to rehabilitation, "In addition to the outstanding secular community organizations assisting in reentry, the faith community of professionals and volunteers is a vibrant and effective group of driven, passionate individuals committed to inhibiting the cycle of recidivism. Research shows that family and community support during and after incarceration significantly helps offenders stay out of prison."[48] The New Hampshire recidivism rate after three years is 43.2 percent, versus the national recidivism rate of 67.8 percent for a three-year period. There are three New Hampshire state halfway houses, the Calumet Transitional Housing Unit, Manchester, and two in Concord, the North End Transitional Housing Unit and the Shea Farm Transitional Housing Unit. Is it possible that the vibrant Christian ministries of Manchester and Concord have contributed to reduced recidivism? Wouldn't it be interesting to consider what the recidivism rate for New Hampshire, and for that matter, the rest of the country would be in the absence of faith-based programs?[49]

Donna Rogers, in her article, "Reentry Programs that Make an Impact," highlights a couple of programs which deserve honorable mention: "The National Reentry Resource Center (NRRC), established by the Second Chance Act and administered by Bureau of Justice Assistance (BJA), is one such resource. It provides education, training, and technical assistance to states, tribes, territories, local governments, service providers, non-profit organizations, and corrections institutions working on prisoner reentry." (More about the Second Chance Act in chapter seven). Rogers goes on to say, "Also, in partnership with the Urban Institute, the Center developed an online resource called the What Works in Reentry Clearinghouse that offers access to research on a variety of reentry programs and practices."[50]

Another leading resource described by Rogers is the evidence-based cognitive behavioral program, Moral Reconation Therapy (MRT). This program has been mentioned to me by some individuals who are residents of Helping Hands, who have attested to beneficial results.

MRT:

> combines education, group and individual counseling, and structured exercises designed to foster moral development in treatment-resistant

clients. Developed by Correctional Counseling Inc., the open-ended interactive group sessions and homework assignments move clients from a hedonistic reasoning level to levels where concerns for social rules and others become important... after completing the program they see success in areas such as: increased housing stability and job retention; reduced substance abuse; decreased hospitalization; increased treatment adherence; and cognitive restructuring that reduces their criminal justice involvement.

Costanza et al. have written an article titled *The Impact of Halfway Houses on Parole Success and Recidivism.* Their findings showed "successful halfway house completion produces short-term and long-term positive effects even in the presence of several other variables that have significant effects on parole completion and recidivism."[51]

Reentry is a vulnerable stage of a former prisoner's life. The halfway house is more regimented than a total release into a home community, and there is frequently a partnership with parole personnel. At the Calumet Transitional Housing Unit, there are parole officers with offices in the building. Halfway houses are simply a sensible buffer, a gradual acclimation opportunity, and vital to these men. Yet they need all the help they can get.

In his book *When Prisoners Return,* Pat Nolan advocates for Christians to be involved in the lives of prisoners returning to the community. He writes,

> As the Church comes alongside returning pris-
> oners, we can help provide or link them with
> valuable practical resources to get back on their
> feet. But most important, the Church can
> manifest the love of Christ to these ex-prisoners
> and help them become ambassadors for Christ
> who are grounded in God's Word, dependent
> on prayer, anchored in the local church, expe-
> riencing freedom from destructive habits, and
> living out the calling to be salt and light in their
> families and communities.[52]

Yes, the phrase "freedom from destructive habits" resonates
powerfully. I have confidence in the church and the love of
God, yet am distressed by the extent of the deep-seated problems of drug and alcohol addiction in the city of Manchester,
New Hampshire. Nolan restores hopefulness as he writes,
"Most people can remember a teacher, coach, or neighbor who
believed in them and helped them believe in themselves. That
is exactly what returning offenders need, yet most have never
had someone like that in their lives. This is where my ministry
brothers and sisters are taking part. And maybe you can, too.

CHAPTER 6

THE LORD AND THE PRISONER

A love for God brings about a longing to know the LORD, and to seek out where in the world the LORD reveals Himself. He has revealed Himself in many ways: through creation, through the history of dealing with mankind, through our LORD Jesus Christ, and through His Word in the Bible. We take "the Word of God" to be the Word of God based on faith and claims made in Scripture itself. The Bible is comprised of various forms of writing: history, poetry, wisdom literature and prophecy. A study of God's Word in each of its forms reveals God's desire for people living today. When we love the LORD, we study the Bible in order to know how God wants us to live.

Another reason we study the Bible is to know the LORD Himself, which involves considerations of *Theology*, defined by *The American Heritage Desk Dictionary* as: "(1) The systematic study, through reason based on faith, of the nature of God and of man's relation to God, (2) An organized theory, system, or body of opinion concerning this study, esp. one belonging to a particular religion."[53] While considering "the nature of God and man's relation to God," let us concentrate on the prisoner and former prisoner. The following pages represent biblical instances of people in and out of prison, with a theological investigation of the LORD's statements and responses to these circumstances.

CHARACTERISTICS OF THE LORD

Before examining God's heart for the prisoner, some consideration of the LORD's characteristics would be helpful. In Exodus, there is an account of the encounter of Moses before God when he was asked to bring a new pair of stone tablets. Moses smashed the first pair, when he saw the people had molded and worshipped a golden calf.

> Then Moses rose early in the morning and went up Mount Sinai, as the LORD had commanded him; and he took in his hand the two tablets of stone. Now the LORD descended in the cloud and stood with him there and proclaimed the name of the LORD. And the LORD passed before him and proclaimed, "The LORD, the LORD God, merciful and gracious, longsuffering, and abounding in goodness and truth" (Exodus 34:4-6).

This is the LORD describing Himself as "abounding in goodness and truth" according to the New King James version of the Bible. The New American Standard version uses the words "lovingkindness and truth." These two descriptions are powerful characteristics which provide insight into the personality of our LORD God. The Hebrew term for these two major traits are pronounced *kesed* {kheh'-sed} meaning: goodness, kindness, faithfulness;[54]and *emeth* {eh'-meth}, meaning: firmness, faithfulness, truth, sureness, reliability, stability, continuance, faithfulness, reliableness; truth as spoken, of testimony and judgment, of divine instruction; truth as a body of ethical or religious knowledge; true doctrine, in truth, truly.[55]

The New Testament parallel description of God's character is seen in John 1:14: "And the Word became flesh and dwelt among us, and we beheld His glory, the glory as of the only begotten of the Father, full of *grace and truth*." Jesus is attributed the same two characteristics as lovingkindness and truth, and the Greek term for "grace" is used, instead of the Hebrew term *khes'sed*. The Greek term is:

charis {khar'-ece} meaning: 1) grace 1a) that which affords joy, pleasure,
delight, sweetness, charm, loveliness: grace of speech 2) good will, lovingkindness, favour 2a) of the merciful kindness by which God, exerting his holy influence upon souls, turns them to Christ, keeps, strengthens, increases them

in Christian faith, knowledge, affection, and kindles them to the exercise of the Christian virtues 3) what is due to grace 3a) the spiritual condition of one governed by the power of divine grace 3b) the token or proof of grace, benefit 3b1) a gift of grace 3b2) benefit, bounty 4) thanks, (for benefits, services, favours), recompense, reward.[56]

The truth of God permeates all of God's Word and provides confidence, faith, and reliability. However, *it is another attribute of God which will receive our attention – lovingkindness.* The Hebrew description of lovingkindness becomes the Greek term for grace, and these descriptions are synonymous for God the Father and Jesus Christ. Lester J. Kuyper writes, "John makes reference to the beginning and creation, and to Moses and the Law, as well as allusion to seeing God – or rather to the fact that no one has seen God at any time. When, therefore, John declares that the incarnate Word is full of grace and truth he is telling his readers to look for meaning of this expression in the Old Testament, where it is descriptive of God."[57]

Iulian Faraonu states, "Fundamentally, 'hesed' means undeserved favor, friendship, praise, as well as God's grace and mercy (Bultmann 1982: 477-484). Therefore, the word goes beyond mere sympathy with and regret for the human needs, and shows God's free and gracious closeness to man."[58] This "free and gracious closeness to man" is monumental over against the lack of mutual affection extended by people, as the psalmist points out:

> The LORD looks down from heaven upon the
> children of men,
> To see if there are any who understand, who
> seek God.
> They have all turned aside, they have together
> become corrupt;
> There is none who does good,
> No, not one. (Psalm 14:2-3)

In spite of the cold-heartedness of mankind, the LORD acts out of compassion.

Faraonu continues, "As the Almighty and Holy God is concerned with the self-induced situation of man, who has so many needs, He sees the misery of a poor suffering man, listens to his complaints, comes down to man's level, so as to know his sorrows and, despite all human infidelity, He accepts man again and, although he would be worthy of punishment, is forgiven and given a second chance."[59] The LORD is the LORD of second chances. The prisoner who is released is in need of a second chance, and halfway houses are the places where this second chance is sorely needed. This description of God, His lovingkindness, or grace, or khes'sed (*hesed*) is the overwhelming characteristic which speaks to the heart of the LORD, the love and concern He has for the prisoner and former prisoner!

THE SERVANT, BONDSERVANT, SLAVE, CAPTIVE, PRISONER

The heart that the LORD has for the prisoner has existed from the beginning. Zach Sewell writes, "Loneliness, disconnectedness, frustration, and loss of precious time in prison are nothing new for God. People have been bound by these elements for centuries. God has worked before in the lives of the imprisoned and will continue to do so."[60] The first mention of the word *prisoner* is found in Genesis 39:20: "Then Joseph's master took him and put him into the prison, a place where the king's *prisoners* were confined. And he was there in the prison." The Hebrew term for the prison itself is: *bayith* {bah'-yith}, which has a simple meaning:)1) house, dwelling, habitation; (2) place; (3) receptacle; (4) home, house as containing a family; (5) household.[61] Coincidentally, the term for *dungeon* is the same as that for *prison,* bayith {bah'-yith}. The Hebrew term for prisoners is *aciyr* {aw-sere'} meaning: prisoner, captive, bondman.[62] This account involves Joseph, son of Jacob. But there is an earlier account of the brother of Abram, before Abram was renamed Abraham: "Now when Abram heard that his brother was taken *captive,* he armed his three hundred and eighteen trained servants who were born in his own house, and went in pursuit as far as Dan" (Genesis 14:14).

The term *captive* in Hebrew is *shabah* {shaw-baw'} meaning, to take captive.[63] This is in adverb form, but the term *captive* in noun form is first seen in Exodus 12:29: "And it came to pass at midnight that the LORD struck all the firstborn in the land of Egypt, from the firstborn of Pharaoh who sat on his throne to the firstborn of the *captive* who was in the dungeon." There, the *noun* for captive in Hebrew is *shebiy* {sheb-ee'} meaning: (1) captivity, captives (1a) (state of) captivity.[64] These terms share the same root.

The first use of the term *slave* is seen in Genesis 43:18, where the brothers of Joseph were nervous about Joseph's motive for calling them back: "he may make a case against us and seize us, to take us as *slaves* with our donkeys." This Hebrew term is *ebed* {eh'-bed} meaning (1) slave, servant; (1a) slave, servant, manservant; (1b) subjects; and used as an adverb indicates servant, manservant, bondman, bondage, bondservant.[65] A slave is not the same as being a prisoner, except in the important component of bondage. Bondage is a trait common to both the slave and the prisoner.

The first mention of the term *prisoner* in the New Testament is found in the Gospel of Matthew, where Jesus was turned over to the Roman governor Pontius Pilate: "Now at the feast the governor was accustomed to releasing to the multitude one *prisoner* whom they wished." (Matthew 27:15). The Greek term for prisoner is *desmios* {des'-mee-os}, meaning bound, in bonds, a captive, a prisoner.[66] The slave is seen as in bondage, and the prisoner is often literally in bonds. The Hebrew term for slave can indicate *bondservant*, which has interesting use in the New Testament: "*Bondservants*, be obedient to those who are your masters according to the flesh, with fear and trembling, in sincerity of heart, as to Christ" (Ephesians 6:5). In

the first chapter of Philippians, Paul and Timothy are described as bondservants to Christ, and in the second chapter, Jesus Himself is described as a bondservant. The term is
also used in Colossians 3:22, 4:1, 4:12; Titus 2:9, and Jude
1:1. The Greek term is *doulos* {doo'-los} meaning (1) a slave,
bondman, man of servile condition; (1a) a slave; (1b) meta-
phorically, one who gives himself up to another's will, those
whose service is used by Christ in extending and advancing
His cause among men; (1c) devoted to another to the disregard of one's own interests; (2) a servant, attendant.[67] In
Matthew 20:26-27, there is use of both of the terms *servant*
and *slave.* "Yet it shall not be so among you; but whoever
desires to become great among you, let him be your *servant.*
And whoever desires to be first among you, let him be your
slave. The *servant* reference is the Greek term *diakonos* {dee-
ak'-on-os} meaning (1) one who executes the commands of
another, especially of a master, a servant, attendant, minister; (1a) the servant of a king; (1b) a deacon, one who, by
virtue of the office assigned to him by the church, cares for
the poor and has charge of and distributes the money col-
lected for their use; (1c) a waiter, one who serves food and
drink.[68] The slave reference is the Greek term doulos {doo'-
los}, which is identical to the term used as bondservant. The
differing use of the terms is ascertained by context.

These terms represent a sliding scale of varying degrees of
bondage. This scale is indicative of a person existing in subjugation to another or others. The range of scale varies from servant
to bondservant, to slave, to captive, to prisoner.

PEOPLE ARE RELUCTANT TO EXIST IN SUBJUGATION TO
SOMEONE ELSE! NO ONE LIKES TO BE DOMINATED.

CHAINS AND PRISON

Another term deserves recognition in relation to the plight or condition of the prisoner. That term is *chains*. The mention of chains in the Old Testament begins in Exodus 28:14, where chains made of gold are fashioned for articles in the tabernacle of the Tent of Meeting and garments for the high priest. These references are either the Hebrew terms (*sharsherah*) meaning chain; or sharshah {shar-shaw'} also meaning chain.[69] In Psalm 107:14, there is gratitude expressed to the LORD for redeeming those who wandered in the wilderness: "He brought them out of darkness and the shadow of death, and broke their *chains* in pieces." This term for chains takes on a new meaning: *mowcer* {mo-sare'} (also in plural *mocerah* {mo-ser-aw'}) meaning band or bond.[70] These chains are chains of bondage, similar to the use of the term *chains* in Isaiah, where the LORD describes a prophetic role of some of Israel's enemies: "They shall walk behind you, they shall come over in *chains*; and they shall bow down to you" (Isaiah 45:14). This is the Hebraic term *ziyqah* {zee-kaw'}; meaning (1) spark, missile, firebrand, flaming arrow; (2) fetters.[71] Jeremiah is described as "bound in *chains* among all who were carried away captive from Jerusalem and Judah, who were carried away captive to Babylon" (Jeremiah 40:1). This term, *aziqqiym* {az-ik-keem'} meaning (1) chains or manacles,[72] is a variation of *ziyqah* {zee-kaw'}. King Jehoahaz of Judah is described as taken prisoner to Egypt: "And they brought him with *chains* to the land of Egypt" (Ezekiel 19:4). This Hebrew term for *chains* is *chach* {khawkh} (or in Ezekiel 29:4) *chachiy* {khakh-ee'}, meaning hook, ring, fetter, brooch.[73]

The first mention of *chains* in the New testament refers to the demon-possessed Gaderene "who had his dwelling among the tombs; and no one could bind him, not even with *chains*, because he had often been bound with shackles and *chains*. And the *chains* had been pulled apart by him, and the shackles broken in pieces; neither could anyone tame him" (Mark 5:3-4). In Greek, the term for *chains* is *halusis* {hal'-oo-sis}, meaning (1) a chain, bond by which the body or any part of it (hands, feet) is bound.[74] The coinciding term for *shackles* is pede {ped'-ay} meaning (1) a fetter or shackle for the feet.[75]

Peter was in prison in Acts 12. "And when Herod was about to bring him out, that night Peter was sleeping, bound with two *chains* between two soldiers; and the guards before the door were keeping the prison" (verse 6). Peter was soon freed from prison by an angel in this account, and the identical term for *chains, halusis* {hal'-oo-sis} is used. Paul and Silas were also freed from prison, this time by an earthquake: "Suddenly there was a great earthquake, so that the foundations of the prison were shaken; and immediately all the doors were opened and everyone's *chains* were loosed" (Acts 16:26). This Greek term for *chains* differs from the one previously mentioned; it is *desmon* {des-mon'} or *desmos* {des-mos'}, meaning a band or bond.[76] *The Greek term for chains is desmos; for prisoner is* δέσμιος *desmios.* The concept of *chains* and *prisoner* are of course closely linked, and there is an English language counterpart concept referring to the prisoner working crews of yesteryear doing road construction. They were nicknamed *chain gangs.* This vernacular is understood to refer to prisoners. In Acts 16:26 we see the term *prison* itself: desmoterion {des-mo-tay'-ree-on}, meaning a prison or a jail.[77] In Greek, we have *chains,* (desmos {des-mos'}); *prisoner,* (desmios {des'-mee-os}); and *prison,* (desmoterion {des-mo-tay'-ree-on}). The English equivalent could be seen as *bonds, the bound, or the place of the bound.*

Paul is mentioned in reference to *chains* in Acts 20:23, 23:29, 26:29 and 26:31 with the Greek term desmos {des-mos'}. The previously mentioned Greek term for *chains,* halusis {hal'-oo-sis} was used in Acts 12:6. In Acts 22:5 there is a third term for *chains:* deo {deh'-o}, meaning (1) to bind, tie, fasten; (1a) to bind, fasten with chains, to throw into chains.[78]

The Apostle Paul was frequently a prisoner for the Lord. He wrote four epistles or letters while in prison: Ephesians, Philippians, Colossians, and Philemon. The book of Acts includes some of his other imprisonments. Paul frequently refers to the term *chains.* He calls himself "an ambassador in *chains* (Ephesians 6:20); describes himself as "in my *chains* and in the defense and confirmation of the gospel" (Philippians 1:7); explains, "it has become evident to the whole palace guard, and to all the rest, that my *chains* are in Christ" (Philippians 1:13);

refers to "my *chains*" again and again: (Philippians 1:14, 1:16; Colossians 4:18; Philippians 1:10; 1:13); and "in *chains*" in Colossians 4:3. Paul is in chains *on purpose with purpose*. He states, "Remember that Jesus Christ, of the seed of David, was raised from the dead according to my gospel, for which I suffer trouble as an evildoer, even to the point of *chains*; but the word of God is not chained. Therefore, I endure all things for the sake of the elect, that they also may obtain the salvation which is in Christ Jesus with eternal glory" (2 Timothy 2:8-10). Paul is willingly in *chains* in his service to the LORD, and he uses a brilliant metaphor in this passage: *"but the word of God is not chained."* The Word of God and the power of the Holy Spirit is not chained and brings about victory and deliverance from chains.

Paul describes himself as a bondservant (Romans 1:1, 2 Corinthians 4:5, Galatians 1:10, Philippians 1:1, Titus 1:1). So does James (James 1:1), Peter (2 Peter 1:1), and Jude (Jude 1:1). These apostles are exemplifying the teachings of Jesus: "whoever desires to become great among you, let him be your servant. And whoever desires to be first among you, let him be your slave" (Matthew 20:26-27). As mentioned earlier, people do not like living in subjugation to others. Yet, in the case of serving God, we understand Him as being our LORD. When we understand the way we should live in service to the LORD, we realize that we are to serve others, *because* we are servants or bondservants of the LORD.

Paul also refers to himself as "the prisoner of the LORD" (Eph 4:1); "the prisoner of Christ Jesus for you Gentiles" (Eph

3:1); "a prisoner of Christ Jesus" (Philemon v.1); "a prisoner of Jesus Christ" (Philemon v. 1:9); and refers to Andronicus and Junia (Romans 16:7), Aristarchus (Colossians 4:10), and Epaphras (Philemon v. 23) as fellow prisoners. The early followers of Jesus Christ were willing to be servants, serving by sharing the gospel, and being willing to become prisoners out of love for the LORD. But those who are imprisoned for sharing their faith in Jesus Christ are *unjustly* imprisoned! How does the LORD want us to respond to those who are justly imprisoned for crimes against others? We have already seen the admonition of Hebrews 13:3: "Remember the prisoners as if chained with them – those who are mistreated – since you yourselves are in the body also."

HOW DOES THE LORD FEEL ABOUT PRISONERS?

The Psalms provide insight into the mind and heart of God. Psalm 68 describes God this way: "A father of the fatherless, a defender of widows, is God in His holy habitation. God sets the solitary in families; He brings out those who are bound into prosperity (verses 5-6). Israelites who travelled through the wilderness are mentioned in this Psalm, but the application of the LORD's concern applies for all time. The word used for "God sets the solitary in *families*" is better interpreted as *house*, (*bayith* {bah-yith} meaning house, dwelling, habitation).[79] God sets the solitary in a house or home, and he brings out those who are bound into prosperity! This is great encouragement to those who have been released into a halfway house. The LORD is saying through this psalm that he is looking out for them.

Psalm 69 expresses this same theme, "For the LORD hears the poor, and does not despise His prisoners" (v. 33). The LORD's compassion extends to the poor and the prisoner. The negative phrase "does not despise" has a reverse meaning, which could be understood as "does not despise, as you might expect, but rather extends His compassion toward" the prisoner.

The author of Psalm 79 appeals to the LORD: "Let the groaning of the prisoner come before You; according to the greatness of Your power preserve those who are appointed to die" (v. 11). This appeal is responded to almost word for word in Psalm 102: 18-20.

> This will be written for the generation to come,
> That a people yet to be created may praise the LORD.
> For He looked down from the height of His sanctuary;
> From heaven the LORD viewed the earth,
> To hear the groaning of the prisoner,
> To release those appointed to death.

The LORD hears the groaning of the prisoner especially when the prisoner is crying out to Him! Psalm 34 emphasizes that, "The LORD is near to those who have a broken heart and saves such as have a contrite spirit" (v. 18). The LORD is *near* those who have a broken heart, *near* those who groan as prisoners, *near* those who have been newly released from prison and feel isolated, or solitary.

Jesus describes the separation of sheep and goats upon His return in Matthew 25: 34-36. "Then the King will say to those on His right hand, 'Come, you blessed of My Father, inherit the kingdom prepared for you from the foundation of the world: for I was hungry and you gave Me food; I was thirsty and you gave Me drink; I was a stranger and you took Me in; I was naked and you clothed Me; I was sick and you visited Me; I was in prison and you came to Me.'" Jesus went on to say, "Assuredly, I say to you, inasmuch as you did it to one of the least of these My brethren, you did it to Me" (Matthew 25: 40). Jesus is assuredly advocating for prisoners. The LORD takes it personally! He states here that a visit with a prisoner means so much to Him that it is like the visitor is lifting the spirit of Jesus Himself!

The statement in Hebrews 13:3 provides a powerful image for the mind's eye: "Remember the prisoners as if chained with them—those who are mistreated—since you yourselves are in the body also." In context, the letter to the Hebrews is addressing the persecution and imprisonment of fellow Christian believers, which the writer of Hebrews had experienced: "for you had compassion on me in my chains" (Hebrews 10:34). One of the blessings of God's Word is that there is application to both the contemporary audience and Christians down through the centuries. Christians, churches, ministries – are to "remember the prisoner as if chained with them." This represents the lovingkindness of God.

The Bible, as we have seen, is composed of different forms of writing: poetry, prophecy, wisdom literature, and much history. The people of biblical accounts were once living. Many of these people experienced life as a captive, a slave or prisoner. The intent of Scripture is for us to learn from the historic figures of God's Word and apply the insights gained in order to benefit those who struggle today with a prison experience.

CHAPTER 7

LIFE AT HALFWAY HOUSES

The Calumet Transitional Housing Unit (halfway house) in Manchester is specifically a New Hampshire state prison release location, intended as a point of reentry into society. The Department of Corrections refers to it as

CALUMET TRANSITIONAL HOUSING UNIT, 126 LOWELL STREET
- Capacity: 64 Males
- Population on January 1, 2018 – 72
- Work release, Furlough program, Educational study release
- Minimum 13 employees[80]

It will be helpful to define what a halfway house is, with some brief historical background. *A Dictionary of Psychology* describes a *halfway house* as "A residential center offering

temporary accommodation and rehabilitation to people recently released from prison or recovering from a mental disorder not requiring full hospitalization."[81] *Britannica Academic*
uses this description:

> Halfway house, also called residential treatment
> center, term that is used to refer to communi-
> ty-based facilities that have been set up to pro-
> vide access to community resources and offer
> transitional opportunities for individuals who
> are attempting to return to society as healthy,
> law-abiding, and productive members of the
> community after they have been found guilty
> of some crime.[82]

M. J. McGowan mentions, "Little is certain about the true
origins of penal halfway houses, but many agree that Christian
monks created their distant cousin in England during the
first century by providing shelters for inmates, whose release
the monks secured from the Crown."[83] It is reassuring that
Christian compassion so frequently typifies humanitarian outreach. "Over the following centuries, religious groups administered similar facilities that focused primarily on providing food
and shelter for socially maligned former convicts."[84]

Halfway houses are "predicated upon the ideals of hu-
manitarianism, rehabilitation, and reintegration. More often
referred to as 'residential treatment centers' in contemporary
criminal justice and social service systems, halfway houses have

been inextricably linked to the dominant punishment philosophy of their eras." Punishment philosophy has never completely gone away and is still considered the main ingredient or purpose for incarceration today.

McGowan points out that "Massachusetts first concocted an American concept of halfway houses in the early nineteenth century," proposing "a halfway house facility in 1817 as a method of combating alarmingly high recidivism rates,"[85] but it was not supported by lawmakers. "For the next century or so only advocacy groups, usually religious ones, called for transitional reentry centers. Some, particularly the Quakers, opened small facilities in cities like New York, Boston, and Philadelphia that welcomed criminals post release."[86] The needs of former prisoners were becoming recognized. "Originally housing the homeless and the poor, by 1845 facilities such as New York City's Isaac T. Hopper House had become popular resources for convicted offenders, as they provided prerelease opportunities for individuals to return to society through a structured program with supportive staff members."[87]

As part of the history of the halfway house in the early part of the nineteenth century, "correctional philosophy in Europe and the United States was dominated by the deterrence theory… Punishment applied with certainty, swiftness, and proportionate severity, it was believed, would deter offenders from further criminal activities." This eventually led to a new paradigm of "positivism" in the twentieth century. The scientific expert was more respected and there was more "belief in rehabilitation of 'sick' offenders rather than the punishment of 'rational' actors."

In the 1930s, a "medical model" of corrections was developed, relying upon classification, diagnosis, and treatment, with the new correctional ideas of probation, indeterminate sentencing, and parole. "As they became further integrated with the former correctional system, eventually becoming the primary prerelease opportunities for inmates, these programs were often characterized as "halfway out of prison" programs." These programs became more specialized in the 1950s, especially with regard to criminally involved drug and alcohol abuse. Deinstitutionalizing of the mentally ill took place during the turbulent 1960s. In the forward to *The Halfway House: On the Road To Independence,* Dr. Allen Frances, a professor of psychiatry, attributes this deinstitutionalizing era as follows: "The discovery of psychotropic medications 30 years ago encouraged a massive movement away from inpatient hospitals, but the patients were usually forced to fend for themselves with inadequate support."[88] Dr. Frances is writing about mental health halfway houses, but the experience for correctional halfway houses is quite similar. "Rehabilitation demands a wide spectrum of services from all levels of the environment."

The 1960s were a time of rehabilitation hopefulness:

> Former United States Attorney General Robert
> F. Kennedy led the first nationwide crusade for
> pre-release community rehabilitation centers…
> In 1961, the ill-fated United States Attorney
> General and First Brother could not have
> seemed more optimistic about the potential for

these, as he formally dubbed them, "pre-release guidance centers" to become a central part of a modern corrections landscape. Kennedy proclaimed in a legal journal that the centers were "no longer an experiment" and instead now a proven method "to redirect young lives."[89]

In 1964, "halfway house advocates formed the International Halfway House Association (now the International Community Corrections Association), a key force behind the push for rethinking what it means to rehabilitate criminals. Then came the Federal Prisoner Rehabilitation Act of 1965, which for the first time authorized halfway houses for adults, among other things." This was a time of U. S. government hopefulness in the cause of reducing recidivism. "White House endorsement of the movement in 1967 only further propelled the proliferation of halfway houses across the country."

The history and development of the halfway house includes a short-lived golden era of the reintegrative ideal during the 1960s and the 1970s because of rising crimes rates, conservative politics, and a growing sentiment for punishment. In 1974, Robert Martinson wrote the article "What Works? Questions and Answers About Prison Reform," in which he pointed out that "with few and isolated exceptions, the rehabilitative efforts that have been reported so far have had no appreciable effect on recidivism."[90] The rate of recidivism remains distressingly high in the twenty-first century, with three out of four returning to prison within five years.

The McGowan article also expresses a bleak outlook on the effectiveness of halfway houses. "Today, one might say that the jury is in: halfway houses do not definitively help or hurt recidivism rates. In other words, they are a wash from the standpoint of preparing their residents for a second chance in society." Kennedy "was correct about the potential of halfway houses, but he was incorrect about their effectiveness as they would take shape in the United States."[91] S. D. Mitchell is more hopeful: "Halfway houses have long been recognized, even by the Bureau of Prisons, as a tool for reentry. Inmates that are not transitioned back to society via a halfway house are more likely than their halfway house counterparts to re-offend."[92]

McGowan describes, "Halfway houses come in a variety of forms, but they can generally be put into three categories: (1) centers focused on mental health recovery; (2) centers focused on drug and alcohol addiction; and (3) facilities providing temporary shelter to criminals learning to reengage with society." Helping Hands Outreach Center of Manchester, New Hampshire, where I serve as chaplain, is a transient housing facility, and has been nicknamed "a three-quarter house." More than two-thirds of the residents have been in the penal system. Many have also been homeless. Former prisoners quite frequently are homeless, and many also struggle with issues of mental health. The challenging reality is that McGowan's categories frequently overlap, and are happening simultaneously! S. D. Mitchell is another advocate for the need for aid in the reentry process: "Absent adequate attention to transitional services, ex-offenders are often homeless, unemployed, and suffer from untreated substance abuse addictions."

The need for reentry programs continues to be recognized. "Community reentry programs are, after all, philosophically a subset of parole, and parole is alive and well in America. From 1980 to [2016], the number of American parolees under state supervision more than quadrupled."[93] The parole process exists partly because of the cost-per-prisoner savings of community release. "Traditional incarceration cost more than $28,000 per federal inmate in 2010, 9.4% more than it cost to house an inmate at one of the Bureau of Prison's contracting halfway houses."

Rehabilitation for the prisoner should rightfully begin in the prison and continue throughout the reentry process. Kent R. Kerley points out a couple of developments which have been favorable regarding faith and prison programs:

...two key things happened since the mid-1990s that signaled a renewed interest in religion and faith-based prison programs. First was passage of the "charitable choice" provision of the 1996 welfare bill, which allows faith-based organizations that provide social services to compete for federal grants. Second, after assuming office in early 2001, President George Walker Bush, via Executive Order 13199, created the White House Office of Faith-Based and Community Initiatives (OFCBI).[94]

Byron R. Johnson adds, "The 2001 White House report *Unlevel Playing Field* systematically reviewed federal funding and identified the barriers that stand in the way of effective government partnerships with faith- and community-based organizations."[95] The bias that exists against faith-based programs and initiatives was at least acknowledged by the Bush administration. The windows were opened to allow for some fresh air. "In 2003 the U. S. Department of Labor launched Ready4Work, a three-year pilot program to address the needs of ex-prisoners through faith-based and community-based organizations. Ready4Work placed an emphasis on job training, job placement, case management, mentoring, and other aftercare services," and "purposely targeted participants with a high probability of recidivism." The results of this three-year trial were researched by Public/Private Ventures, which reported that "only 2.5 percent of Ready4Work participants were reincarcerated within six months, and 6.9 percent were reincarcerated at the one-year post-release mark… Ready4Work gives us an important initial snapshot of what is possible when an intermediary brings together public and private partnerships to address prisoner reentry in a comprehensive and coordinated strategy.

The glimpse of possibilities demonstrated by Ready4Work led to the Prisoner Reentry Initiative (PRI), announced by President Bush in 2004. "Thirty PRI grantees across the country provided mentoring, employment, and other transitional services to thousands of ex-inmates," "results are promising," according to Johnson.

Edward J. Latessa advocates increasing the use of half-way houses. "Although halfway houses are not a panacea, they can provide longer term transitional housing, assist offenders in obtaining employment, and allow them to save some money before release, and to otherwise get back on their feet. Unfortunately, there are not nearly enough halfway houses to handle the number of offenders who require these services."[96] Latessa acknowledges the contribution of faith-based resources:

> Historically, many of the halfway houses and prisoner transition programs were started by charitable and faith-based groups. Many faith-based organizations such as Volunteers of America and Salvation Army have been assisting homeless offenders for many years, but it appears that there is considerable room for more involvement from additional faith-based organizations. Given the recent interest by the Federal Government of expanding and funding faith-based organization, I can think of no better area than assisting in the transitional care of prisoners returning to society.

The U.S. government has continued to acknowledge the need for aid in the reentry process, and in April 2008, The Second Chance Act was established.

> The U.S. Department of Justice announced more than $28 million in grant funding to states, local governments and non-profit organizations under the Second Chance Act Prisoner Reentry Initiative. Funding, awarded through five separate grant programs, will be used to support reentry programs that assist individuals' transition from prison back into the community through a variety of services such as mentoring, literacy classes, job training, education programs, substance abuse, rehabilitation and mental health programs for adult and juvenile offenders.[97]

The Second Chance Act was being deliberated in congress during 2007. During its development, Christy A. Visher writes, "Corrections agencies cannot continue to shoulder the entire burden of preparing men and women to return to communities and lead productive lives. The Second Chance Act recognizes the need for state and local coordination among many actors, including social services, housing, child support, health, education, business, and the faith community."[98] Visher is not singling out faith-based programs in this instance, but she is advocating for the faith community to be part of the overall aftercare of released prisoners.

"Congress also recommended that the Bureau of Prisons use the maximum amount of time allotted for halfway house placement as an incentive to encourage inmates to take

advantage of reentry programming. Congress further recognized that the federal reentry initiative should tailor reentry programs to the individual and not consider reentry as a
one-size-fits-all approach."[99] Any tailoring of programs that is
actually accomplished is frequently upon the shoulders of un-
derpaid, overworked parole officers, who sometimes are more
concerned with keeping the parolee in line.

"The overall purpose of the Second Chance Act was to reduce recidivism and to increase public safety. In an effort to
address these dual concerns at the federal level, Congress dedicated a section in the Second Chance Act to improving federal reentry initiatives and providing incentives to prisoners to
participate in reentry skill development." The Calumet halfway
house of Manchester, New Hampshire has no direct skill development programs, yet the city has a vast array of resources
and job placement. One example of a Christian job placement
ministry is Rise Up Staffing, which matches local businesses
that have work projects with laborers who need paid work.
Lunches and rides to and from the jobs are provided!

The contemporary status of halfway house programs is described by *Britannica Academic* as demonstrating "remarkable
functional flexibility," but the ongoing punishment mentality
of many authorities causes the local state halfway house to be a
strict disciplinarian:

> They adapted to serve the role of alternatives
> to incarceration, and in this capacity, they were
> known as "halfway-in houses." In the 1990s

the term *halfway house* was replaced by the more benign, descriptive, and inclusive *residential treatment centers*. In the 21st century both terms continued to be in use. These adaptations, however, came with a cost, as the treatment orientation of the traditional halfway houses became secondary to concerns about supervision and control. In these new halfway houses, according to a 1992 study, although there was still "counseling, substance abuse treatment, educational and vocational training, and a host of social services...the atmosphere is closer to that of a minimum-security prison than a rehabilitative community.[100]

Charles Samuels, former director of the United States Federal Bureau of Prisons, testified before the House of Representatives, stating, "We use residential reentry centers (RRCs) – also known as community corrections centers or halfway houses – to place inmates in the community prior to their release from custody in order to help them adjust to life in the community and find suitable post-release employment. These centers provide a structured, supervised environment and support in job placement, counseling, and other services."[101] The director pointed out "RRCs [Residential Reentry Centers] are most effective, in terms of recidivism reduction, for higher-risk inmates, especially those who have demonstrated a willingness to participate in education, vocational training, and treatment programs while they are in BOP [Bureau of Prisons] institutions."

There is no doubt that residential reentry centers, or halfway houses, provide the opportunity for a proper readjustment to society, when combined with counseling and rehabilitation programs. The issue becomes the extent of time spent with limited resources.

A report from *The Washington Post* by Joseph Davidson directly points out this concern in its' title "Report: Halfway house issues mean high-risk offenders could be released too soon."[102] Davidson reveals his concern directly in this title. He is responding to a report released by the Department of Justice's Office of Inspector General. The Bureau of Prisons' stated policy of assigning inmates to halfway houses is "based on individual inmate risks and needs, the safety of the community, and available resources." Davidson mentions that the Bureau of Prisons does not always follow this policy, and that low-risk, low-need inmates are far more likely to be placed in halfway houses. Yet, the low-risk inmates might not benefit from the halfway houses to the same extent as "higher-risk inmates who have a strong need for transitional services." At the same time, the space taken by the lower-risk people "increases the likelihood that these high-risk inmates will be released directly into the community when their sentence is completed, without first receiving the benefits of a halfway house." The Bureau of Prisons also has a home confinement program which is included in the inspector general's (IG) report:

There is strong indication that BOP is underutilizing direct home confinement placement as an alternative to RRCs (Residential Reentry Centers, the official term for halfway houses) for low-risk, low-need inmates," according to the IG's office. Yet, it's also the case that some offenders apparently are pushed from halfway houses too soon, "as evidenced by our finding that 17 percent of the 39,020 inmates placed into home confinement during the scope of our audit were subsequently placed back into RRCs for violating home confinement program rules.

The article and the IG report each close with an emphasis upon the importance of supporting successful reentry as means of promoting safer communities. Mitchell agrees, "With the increased focus on reentry and providing inmates with the best opportunity to be successful upon release and the numerous changes in policy, this issue has become one of public interest. Moreover, with the growth of prison populations, halfway houses will become an increasingly important tool for rehabilitation."[103]

The existence of halfway houses has continued to proliferate. "By 1983, the federal government had altogether ceased directly running halfway houses, leaving the task to contracting entities, states, and local governments. Approximately 4,000 convicts lived in about 350 federally contracted halfway houses in 1992. In 2013, according to the Department of Justice, an estimated 30,000 prisoners 'passed through' federally funded halfway houses."[104] This expanded use of halfway houses represents a growing challenge, to address the needs of the rehabilitation process through counseling, mentoring, coaching, and evangelism.

CHAPTER 8

LIFE COACHING

Everyone is not called to do life coaching, but everyone can use some of the principles of life coaching to be a sympathetic listener who encourages a struggling person to establish a plan for the rebuilding of their life. My own parents were the best life coaches, mentors, and counselors I've ever known. They didn't require college degrees or other credentials in order to provide encouragement and inspiration. Degrees and credentials are helpful, but everyday people have a vast God-given capacity to extend lovingkindness toward others. The descriptions of life coaching in this chapter are intended to provide some insight into a process which each of us can use for the benefit of helping others.

I took courses in Transformational Life Coaching at Regent University in Virginia as part of a doctor of ministry program. I approach all learning with a degree of skepticism, wondering at the time whether life coaching really would have traction in the real world. Life coaches are paid well to inspire and encourage people to pursue promotions and greater levels of achievement in the corporate world. But would life coaching fit in with ministering to struggling people? At the time, I was still doing ministry "on the inside," with prisoners at the men's prison in Concord, New Hampshire. I was becoming aware of their trepidation about being released back into the world, and began to realize that life coaching could indeed be specifically helpful for those suddenly faced with a dramatic transition.

This is not a book about life coaching. There are courses and training programs which can lead to certification as a life coach. Life coaching is not the end-all for the needs of the homeless and the former prisoner. But life coaching can be an important "tool in the toolbox," which also includes counseling, mentoring, drug and alcohol rehab, Twelve Step programs, Bible studies, and Christian fellowship.

Life coaching is not the only way to love your neighbor, but it is a practical way of doing so. The roots of the term *coach* stem from horse-drawn wagons and modern buses which were used to help people to get where they wanted to go. "If we look to the origin of the word 'coach', we find that it derives from the word for a 15th century horse drawn transport, first made in the Hungarian village of *Kocs*".[105] Some believe the term may have had an application in the ancient Olympic Games, while others believe the term first arose in the 1880s, "when it was used to identify the person who tutored university students in their rowing on the Cam River in Cambridge [England]."[106] Sports coaching was influenced by the Harvard

University tennis coach Timothy Gallwey who "wrote about 'The Inner Game' combining the practical with the psychological and adding a dimension of self-awareness to coaching practice."[107] Another sportsman and a motor racing champion, Sir John Whitmore, "published his book *Coaching for Performance* in 1992, in which he developed the most influential model of coaching – the GROW model which provided a useful structure for the coaching conversation." The GROW acronym stands for Goal – The Agenda; Reality – The Starting Point; Options – The Possibilities; Will – The Action Steps.[108]

Coaching has not been exclusive to sports. "Over time, the word also became associated with musicians, public speakers, and actors who rely on coaches to improve their skills, overcome obstacles, remain focused, and get to where they want to be."[109] Coaching has also been recognized as important in the corporate business world. According to the February 2000 issue of *Fortune* magazine, coaching became the "hottest thing in management."[110] The International Coach Federation (ICF) was founded in 1992, and has grown to include "thousands of members in approximately ninety countries."[111] Other coaching organizations include Coachville of Great Britain, the European Mentoring and Coaching Council (EMCC), and the Christian Coaches Network. "Only a handful of training programs existed in the late 1990s, but one report estimates that more than 300 exist today." *U. S. News and World Report* has "listed coaching as one of the top ten growing professions and as the second biggest consulting business, second only to management consulting."

Gary R. Collins is an advocate of life coaching. *"Christian coaching is the practice of guiding and enabling individuals or groups to move from where they are to where God wants them to be."* Paul David Tripp points out, "the Bible's view of personal change is radically different from our culture's. Scripture declares that personal transformation takes place as our hearts are changed by God's grace and our minds are renewed by the Holy Spirit. We don't change anyone; it is the work of the Redeemer. We are simply his instruments."[112] Of course life coaches, counselors, mentors, Bible study facilitators and others want to have influence for good in the lives of those they minister to, but "salvation belongs to the LORD" (Psalm 3:8). Tripp goes on to mention, "The overall biblical model is this: *God transforms people's lives as people bring his Word to others."* This is an endorsement for both life coaching *and* evangelism.[113]

Life coaching is a viable conduit for assisting former inmates to find hope and a path forward. The coach yearns to access the motivation located deep inside the heart and soul of the brother or sister being ministered to. Former inmates will carry out steps toward goals if those goals are recognized as their very own unique longings.[114]

The term *client* is used frequently in literature describing the life coaching process. The term is a bit cold and aloof for me, but it is quicker to mention *client* than to use the phrase that fits better in Christian ministry – *the brother or sister being ministered to.*

There is a freedom and flexibility in the coaching process, which reinforces its use in halfway houses with former inmates.

"There is no authorized universal reference manual with standardized diagnoses and coaching solutions neatly defined. Coaching is inherently dynamic."[115] When there is good rapport between coach and client, an environment is established where "it is a good place where clients can tell the whole truth about what they have done, and not done, without worrying about what the coach will say. This is an environment without judgment, and it is a place where the coach expects the truth from the client because truth carries no consequence other than learning, discovery, and new insight."

It is important that clients be the ones to reminisce and talk out their inner thoughts, not coaches.[116] When coaching, coaches are to be fully present for clients. Susan Scott reminds coaches, "Speak and listen as if this is the most important conversation you will ever have with this person. It could be. Participate as if it matters. It does."[117] Curley Martin also emphasizes, "It is really important to stay in the moment, be present and really connected with your client in order to fully understand their experience."[118] This concept of intentional presence is starkly simple, yet of paramount importance. The effectiveness of a good life coach is in their capacity to be an effective listener, and to listen actively, picking up on insights and asking for more when something pivotal is being revealed. "The main role of the life coach is to enable and empower the client."

In my ministry, life coaching has helped people experience personal transformation related to how they see themselves and how they might identify and work toward their goals.[119]

The coach can be that objective listener who picks up on what teachable moments are taking place and can hold that mirror of reflection toward prisoners, former prisoners, homeless people, those struggling with addiction. Life coaching is a valuable asset for those rebuilding their lives.[120]

VISIONS, DREAMS, AND GOALS

The concept of vision in life coaching is vastly important. It is closely related to the pursuit of dreams. Our vision is established through our dreams. Our dreams give us vision. Gary R. Collins insightfully writes a chapter on "clarifying the vision" as he describes, "A vision is a clear picture of something we want to have exist in the future... but anchored in the realities of the present."[121] The realities of the present have a strong hold on former prisoners and homeless people, which is why the pursuit of dreams through a vision of the future, a better future, is paramount for them.[122] Our vision is established through our dreams.

Joseph Umidi frequently emphasizes the life coach's ability to listen. If the client cannot articulate their dream, or have any sense of whether the LORD Himself has a dream for them, it is important for the coach to pick up on the actual dream being described in the coaching conversation. "Once we are hearing others according to how they need to express themselves, then we can help them match God's dreams in them with God's design in them."[123] Tony Stoltzfus acknowledges the importance of dreams as he describes the power of believing in people: "As coaches, we consciously choose to interact with our clients in terms of their destiny, not their problems. We get to know them at a deep level: their dreams, hopes, fears, strengths and weaknesses."[124]

Matthew Kelly recognizes the importance of dreams. "People need someone to help them articulate their dreams, someone to speak with openly about their dreams. It's simple stuff, but it really is powerful."[125] Bruce Wilkinson also gives a high priority to the power of dreams. He has written a modern-day parable or allegory, called *The Dream Giver*, in which he admonishes the reader to "Live out Your Big Dream:" "You are called to go after larger and larger Dreams for God. And He will go with you."[126] Wilkinson asks a powerful question: "Did you have a dream as a child that you lost along the way?" This is worth asking and considering, indeed.

Mark Batterson believes in praying big and dreaming big. In his book *The Circle Maker: Praying Circles Around Your Biggest Dreams and Greatest Fears*, he states, "it is God's faithfulness that increases our faith and enlarges our dreams… God wants you to keep dreaming until the day you die. You're never too old to go after the dreams God has put in your heart."[127]

Talk of dreams is somewhat abstract for former prisoners and homeless people. Their needs are foundational – housing, food, jobs. Their struggles run deep – drug and alcohol addiction, parole requirements, child support payments, lawyer's fees. Considering dreams does seem impractical to those who are struggling. Yet Batterson is on to something when he describes Jesus as honoring "the prostitute who crashed a party at a Pharisee's home to anoint His feet… the tax collector who climbed a tree… the four friends who cut in line and cut a hole in someone's ceiling to help their friend." *This is persistence in prayer and the audacity of dreaming big.* He goes on to say, "The common denominator in each of these stories is holy desperation." And desperation is something that halfway house residents and the homeless *can* identify with. It is frequently harnessed, weighed-down desperation, which many clients will not speak about openly. Proper life coaching does not say, "I told you so" when stirring up thoughts which reveal the existence of desperation. This kind of coaching focuses upon desperation as a motivator for action steps toward goals which lead to actual transformation.

Curly Martin writes, "Life coaching is about gap analysis that closes the gap between life and dreams."[128] Martin values the importance of dreams and is considerate of the obstacles of life. "Life coaching is about removing the obstructions and not adding any new ones."

Coaching in the halfway house setting should not be another required step of the parole process. These men already have enough appointments with treatment programs. Coaching helps "the heart to become alive and awakened to the reality of our true identity, and then allows the coaching process to unbind us and let us live that out in a way that causes the breakthrough."[129] Coaching should properly be about unbinding and breakthrough!

The biggest obstacle these individuals face is the ongoing problem of addiction. There are other hurdles, but this is the biggest. Addiction is the most common *dreambuster*, which is anything which busts your dreams.[130] The concept of a *dream-buster* has been helpful in life coaching sessions. It has traction with the men and women I've spoken to. It is something they can understand, identify, and pinpoint as an enemy, a culprit. It becomes a negative which they can "boot out" of their lives. The coaching process emphasizes remaining positive.

It is important that the client consider what their life purpose is and have a strong vision for their future. Life purpose, vision, and destiny – are topics central to the conversations I have with the people I am coaching, mentoring and providing pastoral counseling to. These concepts are also endorsed by Tony Evans:

> Your destiny without vision is like a surgeon without a scalpel, a cowboy without a horse, or a dancer without a song. Vision gives your destiny inspiration and direction. Trying to discover your destiny without a vision is similar to trying to ignite a fire with a wet match. It won't happen. Having vision is like putting feet to your destiny or putting glasses on a person who suffers from myopia. It enables you to function more fully. It allows you to visualize things and bring them into focus so you can experience them. Your spiritual vision involves *looking further than you can physically see.*[131]

This last line is tremendously memorable, and is a statement that can be identified with and grasped – "Your spiritual vision involves *looking further than you can physically see.* " While sifting in the river for insight and inspiration, we are stumbling upon Tony Evans gold. "Keep in mind that visions bring clarity. And when you receive a clear mental picture of your destiny, you receive power… A clear vision gives you power to make productive and strategic decisions. It also gives you endurance to carry out what is necessary in order to one day reach your vision." Chuck Colsen describes the prisoner as powerless, while Evans demonstrates that a person can receive power through having a vision. This is amazingly helpful to understand for a person trying to put their life together. In life coaching, it is vital to put forward a vision for the importance of *having* a strong vision!

According to Eldin Villafane, "A vision, whether we apply it to an individual or an institution, gives direction, focuses energies, informs content and character, and sets the framework for 'seeing,' and 'valuing' life's true meaning and goals. It shapes the image of self and world."[132] Having a clear vision of what your dreams are helps to conceptualize what your "little g" goals are, and perhaps what your overall "big G" goal in life is too.

The LORD Himself has a goal, as described by Tony Evans: "God's goal is to see His rule and authority cover the earth through the expansion of His kingdom. That is God's purpose in history."[133] An objective review of the entire Bible reveals this to be so. Our best opportunity to establish worthy goals in our lives is to link our goals to the One who created us. Evans writes, "Understanding and embracing God's kingdom is the secret to living with meaning simply because your life is tied to

His kingdom. God's kingdom agenda for you and for all others is based on His comprehensive rule over every area of life."

Instructional material in *The Prison Bible* discusses the importance of setting goals: "Here is an amazing fact: Most people take more time arranging their vacations than they spend planning the rest of their lives! People settle for vague wishes and distant hopes rather than actually making plans and writing down their goals. It is a good thing for Christians to make plans. *It does not show weakness or lack of faith.*"[134] Among the goals outlined in *The Prison Bible i*s this – "You must decide that you will obey *all* the conditions of your parole. Many former inmates end up returning to prison for not following their parole guidelines. You cannot choose which parole conditions you will follow and which ones you will ignore. Avoid the trap of trying to get by with doing as little as possible." First Corinthians 9:26 (ESV) in *The Prison Bible* says "So I run like someone who has a goal. I fight like a boxer who is hitting something."

Goals establish a life plan. Robert E. Coleman reinforces the importance of establishing a life plan as he writes, "What is the plan of your life? Everyone has to live by some plan. The plan is the organizing principle around which the aim of life is carried out."[135]

For my life coaching ministry, I have established a PowerPoint briefing. There is an ongoing interview in order for me to get a sense of the clients' backgrounds and current status, but I do most of the talking as the intention is to give them much to consider. This is followed up by two additional, less formal sessions, during which the clients provide feedback about their dreams and goals. The aim is to have them establish strong goals and an overall life plan, to recognize the current season of their life as a time of rebuilding. For those I have seen at least three times, I provide a Certificate of Achievement, which can be shown to parole offices and others who may want to know what resources and programs the client may be using.

Included at the beginning of the initial briefing are pictures of coach Bill Cowher with Ben Roethlisberger; coach Bill Belichick and Tom Brady; coach *Béla Károlyi* with both Nadia Comaneci and Kerri Strug; coach Claude Julien with Brad Marchand; Ivan Lendl with Andy Murray. The point I make as a coach is that coaches bring out your best. The results of these pairings of coach and athletes have resulted in Super Bowl championships, the first perfect 10.0 in Olympic gymnastic competition, gold medals, a Stanley Cup; and a couple of Wimbledon championships. Transformational life coaching is not sports coaching, but there are parallels. These sports pairings are symbolic of attaining high levels of achievement. Clients are asked, "What is your Super Bowl, your gold medal, your Stanley Cup, your Wimbledon championship?" There are literally goal posts, goal lines, and goals scored in these sports, and the establishment of goals is vital to the coaching process.

One of the important slides which I present at each life coaching briefing has the following series of questions:
- What Do I Want to Do?
- Who Do I Want to Be?
- Who Do I Want to Help?

- What is my Ideal Lifestyle?
- What Do I Value, or Hold Important?
- Can I Remember My Dreams?
- What are My Goals?[136]

This series of questions can be overwhelming to consider all at once, but the process is intentional. I tell the men and women I'm trying to help, "This is one of the main reasons I asked to sit and talk with you." We review each question, and frequently the person I'm trying to help will give a preliminary answer. But I don't force answers. I tell them that it's more important to think these things through. We come back to these questions over the next couple of times we talk. I tell them that the stronger the set of goals that they set for themselves, the more determined they are, the stronger the vision that they have for a rebuilt life, the more likely they will realize their dreams and find joy, hope, blessing, and fulfillment, *with God's help*.

CHAPTER 9

COMPASSIONATE EVANGELISM

My role as chaplain includes intentional evangelism, or the simple encouragement of Christian faith. The word *evangelism* is an English form of the original Greek word *euangelion*, which means "good news message." The word *angel*, or "messenger," is part of the term. The English Bible translates *euangelion* as the term *gospel*. When we read "And Jesus went about all Galilee, teaching in their synagogues, preaching the gospel of the kingdom, and healing all kinds of sickness and all kinds of disease among the people" (Matthew 4:23), the Greek word for 'gospel' is *euangelion*. To evangelize is to bring good news. To evangelize is to share the gospel. I'm sharing with you the gospel truth!

There is no arm twisting when I share my love for God. Other brothers and sisters who provide outreach through the

Christian ministries of our area do so with compassion. We minister to the needs of people, and we share good news as we do so. For those residents of sober living homes who have Christian faith, the process of evangelism is confirming and reassuring. For those who do not have Christian faith, what is offered is the establishment of a lifelong companion who goes with you, and the spiritual understanding that one does not have to go it alone. I encourage fellowship with God through faith in Jesus Christ because a joyful, hopeful, blessed, fulfilling life results from fellowship with God! What the Lord offers is good news! When you need recovery or are in the process of rebuilding your life, there is no better resource than the Lord! Eternal salvation comes in pretty handy as well.

With God's help, halfway house residents and homeless people may thrive and live life more fully. Dallas Willard writes about "the profound needs and hungers of the human soul."[137] Charles Colson brings out a similar concept as he states, "Some knowledge of spiritual truth is in every human heart."[138] He goes on to say, "evangelism should flow naturally out of the context of our everyday lives."

A person who evangelizes is a "witness" for the LORD. A witness in Christian ministry serves from the standpoint of wisdom and spiritual maturity. This takes time, reading and hearing God's Word, and living in connection with Christian fellowship. The Christian witness has a responsibility to be sincere regarding his or her own walk of faith. There is a testimony to offer, not to monopolize the shared conversation, but in order to be open and authentic, and as a way of helping the person they are speaking with to also open up. Reggie McNeal explains that evangelism should not be about churching the un-churched, but about "connecting people to Jesus."[139] A person who is evangelizing aims to allow the person they are helping to consider matters of the heart and soul without dictating princi-ples or preaching. John M. Perkins calls this approach "neigh-boring vs. fixing," and states, "No one likes to be someone's project. But we all like to be considered someone's friend."[140] At the same time, "Competence to provide care and cure for souls depends on a rich and growing familiarity with all that God has revealed, about life and people and what's wrong with us and what He is doing about it."[141]

God is the one in control. "God's sovereignty means that there is nothing that exists beyond God's reign."[142] The LORD exclaims, "I will feed My flock, and I will make them lie down," says the LORD GOD. "I will seek what was lost and bring back what was driven away, bind up the broken and strength-en what was sick" (Ezekiel 34:15-16). Against this backdrop, or rather upon this solid foundation, there is a need for what Kim Hammond and Darren Cronshaw call "safe places," "to nurture faith while avoiding inappropriate and unauthentic evangelism."[143] The method described for doing evangelism in these safe spaces sounds similar to life coaching concepts. "Rather than speaking about what we believe or want to con-vince someone of, we start with questions to find out what they believe and what they have already experienced of God. We want to find out where people are coming from and ask questions that provoke their thinking. Let's plant seeds with questions rather than first giving information." This statement actually describes evangelism as coaching, or is it coaching as evangelism?

The concept of coaching and applying evangelism in a halfway house setting has come about in my ministry through the influence of the Holy Spirit. But coaching is only one way of helping among so many other ways. You might be gifted as a mentor, or as a recovery advocate, or you could facilitate a Bible study. Increasingly, more people are released from the local prison and finding their way into many local Christian ministries. The fear and worry evident in these people is a profound demonstration of how they struggle in an emotional and psychological foxhole. While visiting many newly released former inmates that I knew from prison ministry, I recognized the deep need for support and encouragement during this time of dramatic transition. The 1269 Café hosts Christian worship services on Sundays together with a fellowship dinner. Calumet halfway house is just three blocks away, and many of its residents have lunch at the Café, as do residents of the Helping Hands sober house. The people at this homeless outreach need help as well!

I keep mentioning these places where I'm doing ministry together with Christian brothers and sisters. My hope is that you will recognize the need that exists in your own community or nearby – the halfway houses, sober living homes, and homeless outreaches and programs that could use a helping hand.

Can life coaching, mentoring, and ministering to others be approached in an objective, secular way, without the need for evangelism? Yes! But there is power in the Spirit of the LORD to transform (2 Corinthians 3:18), and the LORD can give you "a new heart and put a new spirit within you" (Ezekiel 36:26). Billy Graham wrote of a priority in the foreword to Robert Coleman's *The Master Plan of Evangelism* – "the priority to reach out in love to a confused and dying world with the good news of God's forgiveness and peace and hope through Jesus Christ."[144] Coleman describes the approach required for doing evangelism in a way which mirrors the approach to coaching as he writes of "the need for a well-thought-through strategy of movement day by day in terms of the long-range goal. We must know how a course of action fits into the overall plan God has for our lives if it is to thrill our souls with a sense of destiny." Evangelism is the action plan and the goal of the life coach, mentor, Bible study facilitator.

The message of Coleman's *The Master Plan of Evangelism* is to copy Jesus, the Master Himself. Ronald J. Sider concurs with Coleman regarding doing evangelism according to the Master, as his title would suggest, *Doing Evangelism Jesus' Way: How Christians Demonstrate the Good News.* Sider makes the case, "Christ has no backup plan; you and I are it. His plan to save the world and change it is not one He decided to carry out through angels. He decided that you and I would do it."[145] The followers of Jesus are called to break the yokes of oppression and bondage.

Life coaching makes use of vision, goals, and the formulating of a plan. For the Christian, the vision, the goals, and the plan include evangelism. Sider describes his understanding of evangelism: "I'm not talking about any certain method. I'm talking about longing and praying for sensitive ways to invite people to confess Jesus Christ as their LORD and Savior. I'm talking about positive ways to invite people into a living relationship with Christ and to join His new community."

People who struggle want to live in new communities, or perhaps they long to live in old communities in new ways. The LORD becomes a companion who sticks with those who have faith in Him. Jesus says, "Behold, I stand at the door and knock" (Revelation 3:20), and a coach or mentor who evangelizes asks, "Is that the LORD I hear knocking at the door of your heart?" Evangelism opens the door to salvation. According to Sider "Salvation includes not just the forgiveness of my sins, but also the way that the Holy Spirit begins to sanctify me as I come into a living relationship with Christ. It doesn't stop there, either! Salvation includes the transforming relationships that arise within the circle of people who accept Christ." The transformation desired is enhanced by the transforming power of the Holy Spirit! "If we believe what the New Testament says about Jesus, then we will want to share Him as rapidly, as eagerly, and as sensitively as we can. We must combine Christian word and deed. We must combine evangelism and social ministry," suggests Ronald J. Sider. The Christian ministries around town which help those that are struggling are undertaken on behalf of social ministry, and they are increased in value as we apply evangelism and rely upon the power of God.

William Powell Tuck also believes in doing evangelism according to the Master. He writes, "Authentic evangelism is patterned after the methods of the Master and his disciples. Authentic evangelism is a way of sharing the Good News that demonstrates respect and concern for the total person with whom the message is communicated."[146] Tuck further mentions, "True evangelism – the saving message of God's grace for all persons – will also be concerned with the social conditions in which people live." My ministry involvements have been initiated as a way to minister to those struggling under the difficult conditions of reentry, to meet people where they are. "As we study the life of Jesus, we observe that Jesus had no set method of evangelism but responded to people where he found them and to whatever their need was." Tuck emphasizes authenticity. Former inmates recognize and respect authenticity. Many have mentioned to me that they learned to "read" others, at first as a defense mechanism, and later as sizing up whether that person was trustworthy. Trust is what genuine Christian witnesses bring to the table.

Robert D. Lupton writes of community development and ministering to the poor. "Evangelism is very much a part of Christian Community Development. The answer to community development is not just providing a job or a decent place to live, but it is also having a true relationship with Jesus Christ. It is essential that the good news of Jesus Christ is proclaimed and that individuals place their faith in Him for salvation."[147] Living an abundant life beyond just a job and a home is what the LORD desires for all of us, as Jesus said in John 10:10.

Timothy Keller writes of the exclusive contribution of "the ministry of the church of Jesus Christ" in mending broken families and attacking "the roots of social problems." "Only Christians, armed with the Word and Spirit, planning and working to spread the kingdom and righteousness of Christ, can transform a nation as well as a neighborhood as well as a broken heart."[148] It is the Holy Spirit's transforming power that enables the brokenhearted and the struggling ex-offender to "be transformed by the renewing of your mind" (Romans 12:2). Keller's book emphasizes *Ministries of Mercy,* and he makes this observation: "Some teach that evangelism has primacy over mercy, meaning that *mercy is a means to the end of evangelism.* That is, we minister to people in deed as a way of bringing them to Christ." Evangelism is deliberately being carried out during our coaching sessions and recovery teaching. Some may come to have faith in Jesus Christ for the first time, but life coaching and recovery teaching will carry on whether or not the halfway house residents have Christian faith. Keller writes of doing good deeds of mercy as modeled by the parable of the good Samaritan, pointing out that "deed ministry, like grace itself, is unmerited favor… First John 3:17 tells us that the motive of any ministry is love. If we see a need, we meet it, if we can. This puts evangelism and mercy on an equal footing motivationally… Word and deed are the proverbial 'two wings of the airplane.' The two wings of Christian ministry done around town represent mercy and evangelism. Mercy and evangelism are at the heart of God.

Former President Jimmy Carter has written a book titled *Faith: A Journey for All,* published in 2018. As a ninety-three-year-old, he shares his personal thoughts regarding evangelism:

After some thought and contemplation of written definitions, I consider myself to be an evangelical Christian. According to my Bible commentary, "Evangelism is the active calling of people to respond to the message of grace and commit oneself to God in Jesus Christ." Wikipedia says that "evangelicals believe in the centrality of conversion or the 'born again' experience in receiving salvation, in the authority of the Bible as God's revelation to humanity, and in spreading the Christian message." The basic elements of Christianity apply personally to me, shape my attitude and my actions, and give me a joyful and positive life, with purpose.[149]

It is the shaping of attitude and actions which Christian ministry intends to influence, with hope for the kind of results that President Carter describes as "a joyful and positive life, with purpose."

The apostle Paul wrote of the challenges of doing evangelism, "But even if our gospel is veiled, it is veiled to those who are perishing, whose minds the god of this age has blinded, who do not believe, lest the light of the gospel of the glory of Christ, who is the image of God, should shine on them" (2 Corinthians 4:3-4). Jesus expressed these same challenges when He said to Nicodemus, a teacher of Israel: "Most assuredly, I say to you, We speak what We know and testify what We have seen, and you do not receive Our witness" (John 3:11). J. I. Packer addresses these challenges as follows:

> Should we conclude that preaching the gospel is a waste of time, and write off evangelism as a hopeless enterprise, foredoomed to fail? No; because the Spirit abides with the Church to testify of Christ. To the apostles, He testified by *revealing* and *inspiring*, as we saw. To the rest of men, down the ages, He testifies by *illuminating*: opening blind eyes, restoring spiritual vision, enabling sinners to see that the gospel is indeed God's truth, and Scripture is indeed God's Word, and Christ is indeed God's Son.[150]

The illuminating capacity of the Holy Spirit is a presence and a power which Christians in ministry continue to rely upon. And the responsibility for a transformed life is also shared with the person who hears the gospel, the *witnessee*. Mark E. Dever reminds us that evangelism, the sharing of "good news," requires repentance. "The repentance that Jesus demands is connected with believing this news, because if it's really 'news,' it's no surprise that you change your mind when you hear it. The word for 'repent' is *metanoia,* and means literally 'to change your mind.'[151] This involves being transformed by the renewing of your mind (Romans 12:2). Dever describes Christianity as "in some radical sense, an about-face. And it's an about-face all Christians make, but only as part of their relying on Christ's work on the cross. To say you trust without *living* as though you do is not to trust in any biblical sense." The stark concept of an about-face is understandable to everyone who has served in the military, and it is understandable to the former prisoner. The depth of the meaning of an about-face is profound. When you say, "Brother, you have to make an about-face," that brother hears you. This concept resonates, it has traction.

Mark E. Dever also asks the question, "Who should evangelize?", which is answered in part by mentioning that all Christians should "always be ready to give a defense to everyone who asks you a reason for the hope that is in you, with meekness and fear" (1 Peter 3:15). Dever advocates that all Christians have a role in evangelism, and he affirms the central role of the church when he writes, "We can all contribute to evangelism simply by building up the local church – helping to organize it or lead it." The British theologian Martin Lloyd Jones also affirmed the church when he wrote, "Evangelism is pre-eminently dependent upon the quality of the Christian life which is known and enjoyed in the church."[152] Wherever you find yourself being involved in ministering to others, it is important to be able to recommend churches in the immediate area, where they can worship and find support and encouragement.[153]

The September 2016 issue of *Christianity Today* magazine contains a couple of "after prison" articles. Morgan Lee describes the plight of those who have served time in prison. "Once released, former prisoners enter a hidden underworld of legalized discrimination and permanent social exclusion. They are members of America's new under-caste."[154] Lee points out the expansion of organizations like Prison Fellowship, adding that "Prison Fellowship is largely alone in its efforts. In spite of the dramatic growth of incarceration, ministries to those in and returning from prison remain a distinct minority of evangelical organizations." *This is the very reason for writing this book of encouragement for people to be involved.* The second *Christianity Today* article: "Our Back-From-Prison Family," by Harold B. Smith, describes a community program in the suburbs of Chicago, known as Radical Time Out (RTO). This ministry provides worship, comfort, testimonies, and dinner for ex-offenders and the mothers, sisters and fathers of many who are still in prison.[155] Pastor Marco David is quoted, "When we step out in faith and love to extend grace to the prisoner, we are joining with Jesus in his radical work of redemption. When we go where Jesus is working, we will encounter his transforming presence and power in ways that will fuel our faith and bring glory to his name."

Jim Buchan, author of *Apostolic Evangelism,* emphasizes the *go* of evangelism. "Although it is wonderful to have services where we can confidently invite unconverted people, that is not the main pattern of the Gospel. God's primary plan is not that the lost would be sent to us, but that we would be sent to them.[156]

The needs of the inner-city cry out for a *Go* ministry. Our LORD Jesus said, "for the Son of Man has come to seek and to save that which was lost" (Luke 19:10). We who follow Jesus, not only try to do as He said, but we should try to do as He *did.*

He said, "Go therefore and make disciples of all the nations, baptizing them in the name of the Father and of the Son and of the Holy Spirit, teaching them to observe all things that I have commanded you" (Matthew 28:18). The great commission is a *Go* commission. And what Jesus did was to seek and save the lost. When you are actively *seeking* those who are lost, you must *Go* where they are. For the sake of eternal fellowship with God our Father, we should witness, we should evangelize while we minister to them with compassion.

CHAPTER 10

A HEART FOR THE HOMELESS OF THE CITY

Many Christians among the ministries of Manchester, New Hampshire, have a heart for the homeless of their city. According to Jack Dennison, "The neighborhoods of your city belong to God. The cities of America belong to God. The nations of the world belong to God. He wants them, and He will have them – every one of them!"[157] Harvey Cox writes, "The Christian faith came to birth in a world of teeming and conflict-ridden cities."[158]

Manchester is certainly conflict-ridden. Below is one lead to a story from April 8, 2018:

HOMELESS TENTS DEMOLISHED CAMPS IN THE CROSSHAIRS I HOMELESS ENCLAVE BULL-DOZED, 2 OTHERS EYED
By MARK HAYWARD

New Hampshire Union Leader

MANCHESTER — With one homeless camp
bulldozed this past winter, city officials say they
are taking steps to eliminate two more camps,
one where a woman said she's been living for
four years and not bothering anyone.[159]

The demolishing of tent camps around the city of
Manchester has happened at other times in recent years.

Another major problem is opioid abuse and addiction. The
city of Manchester, New Hampshire has received national attention extending to the White House. In March 2018 both
the president and the vice president of the United States visited
Manchester. Here are segments from the local news reports:

First lady Melania Trump, Mayor Joyce Craig
and Gov. Chris Sununu joined the President
when the presidential motorcade stopped at
Central Fire Station en route to Manchester
Community College, where Trump gave a
speech detailing his "Initiative to Stop Opioid
Abuse." The stop gave the President a firsthand
look at the Safe Station program.[160]

On Monday in Manchester, Trump rolled
out the administration's strategy to battle the
opioid crisis. Pence saluted Manchester first
responders Dan Goonan, Chris Hickey and

Chris Stawasz, who championed a Safe Station program that's become a national model. "Two years later a program called Safe Station is providing relief to thousands of people. We're all so proud of you," Pence said. The program allows substance users to come to fire stations to seek treatment without fear of arrest.[161]

The troubles of the city of Manchester are reflected in the lives of the men of Helping Hands and the men of Calumet halfway house. The majority of men coming to Helping Hands have been incarcerated, and many of them arrived in a state of homelessness. The men of Calumet have all been released from prison, but homelessness looms in the future for many of them. It is because of these troubles and in spite of them that we are serving the LORD and ministering to these men, and with 1269 Café, men and women.

Robert D. Lupton has a heart for the poor of the city. He acknowledges, "In declining urban communities there is no shortage of need."[162] He describes hands-on ministries such as clothes closets, food pantries and others in an interesting way: "We can describe this kind of personal involvement as 'betterment' activities. Betterment activities offer relief from difficult situations and improve the existing conditions." One of these "betterment" activities is 1269 Café, where there are meals and worship services, Bible studies and Twelve-Step programs. Lupton points out an important factor in ministering to the poor: "People of compassion – often visionary,

mission-minded people, even 'called' people – who are moti-
vated to minister to the poor bring much needed programs,
resources and care to a depleted neighborhood. Yet, as important as these services may be (essential, some would say),
serving people is distinctly different from *developing* people."
This point by Lupton is a grand distinction. He goes on to
say, "Betterment *does for* others; development enables others
to *do for themselves*. Betterment improves conditions; development strengthens capacity." Life coaching for the Calumet
and Helping Hands residents is an intentional attempt to
foster development. These men are housed, fed, clothed and
attend rehab for their betterment. They are being coached for
their development.

Dr. Eldin Villafañe is the founding director of Gordon-
Conwell's Center for Urban Ministerial Education (CUME)
and the former minister of education at the Iglesia Cristiana
Juan 3:16 in the Bronx, New York, at that time the largest
Hispanic church in the nation." [163]

He shares his heart for those of the inner city:

> time and again, I have been driven by God's
> Spirit to find fresh inspiration in the words
> of the prophet Jeremiah: 'And seek the Peace
> [Shalom] of the city... and pray to the LORD
> for it; for in its Peace [Shalom] you will have
> Peace [Shalom]' (29:7).
> I am concerned for the city – particularly the
> inner-city reality that is being shaken by the

mindless violence of its youth and undermined by the cold indifference of institutional violence. I am concerned with a church that has no mind for a wholistic vision for the city.[164]

Eldin Villafañe writes of "the unrestrained, rudderless, and destructive subculture in our cities," and refers to this as "a prophetic manifestation of a people perishing for lack of *a vision*. Individuals and institutions – including the church – that are to model and live out a vision are themselves visionless." Dr. Villafañe is reaffirming the importance of vision which is a strong theme in transformational coaching. In order to minister to people, Christians should have a vision of how this is done, and the halfway house resident could really use a strong vision of where he is going.

During coaching briefings and devotional times at the "housekeeping" meetings of Helping Hands Outreach, I constantly refer to God's desire for joy, hope, blessing, fulfillment, and abundance in the lives of the men. All of these wonderful attributes of the love of God are contained in the concept of the Old Testament term *Shalom*. Professor Eldin Villafañe left an indelible mark of memory for me and many other students of Gordon-Conwell Theological Seminary when he continually referred to this encompassing concept of *Shalom:* "Shalom speaks of wholeness, soundness, completeness, health, harmony, reconciliation, justice, welfare – both personal and social. The church is an instrument, a servant, of peace in the city. It preaches and lives out the Shalom of God."

The men of Calumet halfway house require many resources and opportunities, and life coaching is an important instrument for their path of recovery. It is so important to establish vision and pursue dreams during the coaching process, and it is pivotal to set strong goals. Doing so with faith in the LORD as encouraged by intentional evangelism has been a Godsend for the rebuilding of these men's lives.

Christian Aftercare Ministries has a suite of rooms in the Helping Hands Outreach Center building in Manchester. Their ministries include evangelism, mentoring, and the counseling of halfway house visitors from Calumet and newly released former prisoners from throughout the Southern New Hampshire region. They offer clothing donations, bus passes, tracts, and Bibles. The director, Paul Roussel, and associate, Mike Grady conduct frequent visits and Bible studies at New Hampshire jails and prisons.

PAUL ROUSSEL OF CHRISTIAN AFTERCARE MINISTRIES

BIBLE STUDY LED BY MIKE GRADY (SEATED WITH HAT)

Christian Aftercare Ministries is a proactive Christian presence for the spiritual health of the halfway house residents, Helping Hands Outreach residents, and walk-ins. Mike Grady's weekly Bible studies bring in an eclectic group, most of whom are in recovery. Frequently, someone visits out of gratitude and thanks the Christian Aftercare mentors and me for helping them as overcomers and rebuilders. One of our Helping Hands residents named John paints and does calligraphy. He was kind enough to paint a sign for our hallway, which reads, "Good News Hallway." The good news comes from the people who stop in, and the good news is shared by those of us witnessing for Jesus Christ. What a privilege it is for me to be partnered across the hall with such godly men, with supportive Helping Hands people down the hall, and with ministry friends across the city!

My friend Richard has cerebral palsy. For a few months, he found himself homeless, living in his wheelchair, having difficulty finding places to recharge the wheelchair's battery pack. The following testimony is in his own words:

> I had been in and out of the prison system, doing jail time while at the same time I was doing work for a missions' group, going out and doing street ministry behind the scenes. I worked loading trucks to ship to areas that needed help the most. The missions' group I worked for was Vision International Missions. There I found the Lord and I became ordained. I had gotten in trouble a few years ago and ended up going to prison. When getting out of prison I thought that I would be able to do things differently on my own. I ended up becoming homeless -- about to lose all my friends. It was a quick sense of not knowing what to do. I was out using drugs and alcohol on a daily basis. My attitude had changed for the worst. I was losing the people I have known and loved my whole life. I was told at that point that if I did not change my ways I was not welcome back in their life. I had to make a serious change in my life again. this time I ask the Lord what I needed to do. He told me to go see Paul Roussel at Christian Aftercare Ministry. I went down

and talked to Paul and he introduced me to the people at Helping Hands. I was able to get a room there at Helping Hands. I went back and talked with Paul for a while and we talked about the Lord and I had told him about what had been going on. He asked me if I had been attending church and I told him, "no." I was finally being honest. Since meeting with Paul and getting into Helping Hands I have been able to do so much more with my life. I now go to church on a weekly basis. I have my friends back in my life. I have new friends that I am helping. I'm talking to my brother who I had not talked to in over a decade. I have found the Lord! I let Him in my life again and what I mean by again is I had once pushed Him out of my life. Because the Lord is in my life, all is well today! I talk to the Lord on a daily basis; I listen to what he has to tell me; I read my Bible; I get involved with church activities. I'm clean and I'm sober! I just celebrated 28 months of clean time and that is all due to trusting in the Lord Jesus Christ! And reading the Word of the Lord gives me so much insight on things that I never knew! And I would just like to say that if someone is struggling out there and doesn't know what to do or where to go -- all you have to do is ask the Lord to help you and trust that

Jesus will show you what needs to be done in your life -- like he has in mine! Today I leave my life in his hands. I don't worry about the little things like I used to. If you need help and are unsure how to do this -- all you have to do is talk to someone in your local church, or you can talk to one of us today and we will show you the way to embrace Faith in the Lord. I pray that I may be able to help someone that needs help finding the Lord!

Richard now resides at Gendron House, a sober house apartment building which is an extension of Helping Hands Outreach Center. He proudly embraces the duties of assistant house manager, and loves encouraging the men of both buildings to rebuild their lives.

CHAPTER 11

RECOVERY

In the city of Manchester, New Hampshire – between the Helping Hands Outreach Center (a sober living home), 1269 Café homeless outreach down the street, the Department of Corrections halfway house up the street, and people wandering around *in* the streets – we see so many folks in need of recovery. It should have been no surprise to me, when after teaching and speaking with so many homeless people and then interviewing and doing transformational life coaching with men at both the halfway house and the sober home, that the vast majority were or had been in the clutches of *substance use disorder* (SUD).

Substance use disorder is the latest politically correct, psychologically sensitive, sociologically feasible description. It is considered insensitive to use a phrase like "stuck on drugs and alcohol," or "substance abuse." These characterizations are considered too dangerously close to attaching a stigma to the person with SUD. *No one ministering to people out of love for God wants to stigmatize or bring shame down upon the drug or alcohol user.* Concern for some of the name-calling and unkind labels put on people struggling under the influence of these self-destructive behaviors is a valid one. Yet these *are* self-destructive behaviors! We have not stigmatized the *use* of drugs and alcohol nearly enough! We should work on disarming and eradicating the disorder while helping the individual rebuild their life! Recovery, in the context of addiction, starts with sobriety and is maintained by transformation, by the rebuilding of a life!

I have spent many years taking courses as part of my Master of Divinity degree at CUME (Center for Urban Ministerial Education), at inner city churches around Boston, including courses on drugs and society. I learned as much from colleagues involved in the rough and tumble of street ministry as I did from the professors, who were dedicated also in doing street ministry. I've taken social worker courses along the way which included material on the influence of drug and alcohol abuse on family and loved ones; and took community transformation courses on the way to the Doctor of Ministry degree. I have not been on a credential hunt or stuck on academia – I am seeking a closer connection with the things of God, and yearn to know more about helping others. Along the way, there was a week of training as a "recovery coach." I've read books, seen diagrams and slides on the physiological effects of the brain, neurotransmitters, and the central nervous system. My concern for the needs of the addicted has made me aware of the causes and influence of addiction, *but I'm more interested in the solution to recovery from addiction.*

My only brother, younger by a year and a half, died from liver complications related to alcohol at the age of 58. He never stopped drinking, even after he knew it was killing him. He was surprised, because he said for the most part, "It's only beer." His addiction not only terminated his life, but was a source of strife for many years. He was bitter and angry when he drank, even though I tried to connect him with our kids, his nieces and nephews. We did have great memories growing up in Canada when we were young. Most family members know someone who has been stuck in addiction. You don't have to have an addiction yourself in order to understand the effects it has.

Recovery has become a buzzword for dealing with drug and alcohol addiction. But let's consider an expansion of the understanding of recovery. If you google the word *recovery* you will find two definitions:

1. a return to a normal state of health, mind, or strength
2. the action or process of regaining possession or control of something stolen or lost

According to an expanded understanding, beyond the connection with addiction, we already realize the need for recovery when we've had a surgical procedure, an injury or a medical condition. We are also in need of recovery if a good friend let us down, we lost a job, we went through a divorce, or a loved one passed away. If we've been in the military, did time in prison, or have been homeless for a time, we are in the need of recovery. By this expanded understanding, we all have been in need of recovery and continue to be in recovery. This expanded understanding – beyond the process of healing from addiction – helps people who have not struggled with addiction to identify with the need for some process of recovery. Former addicts can be tremendous advocates for the recovery process of those addicted, but their capacity for care is not exclusive. Everyone can sympathize.

Addiction is so insidious. Often people use drugs or grab a drink when they believe they need an escape from pain or circumstances. The escape becomes a craving. Then they can't seem to escape the escape. When crime is involved, incarceration creates a restricted environment from which they'd like to escape. The influences of addiction have a vast capacity for destruction. The craving of addiction causes the person with substance use disorder to become self-absorbed, or more accurately craving-absorbed. There is little room for being responsible for others; a withdrawal from family ties; a reduced capability to be a steady employee. Even though there is a seeking out of others who are also addicted, the trend is a path toward greater and deeper *isolation*. It's *lonely*. Because of addiction, people have lost businesses, homes, spouses, and connection with family members. They've lost their joy in life and their independence.

Speaking of independence, an addiction is a *dependence*. Ironically, with addiction and life in general, people often react to encouragement in Christian faith as a dependence upon God which they'd rather skip. I've heard many responses along these lines: "Don't give me that God stuff. I don't need him. Let me do my thing. Let me be free to do drugs or get drunk or whatever I want." *This kind of freedom is bondage.* The irony is that the guise of "freedom to do whatever you want" can result in bondage to drugs or alcohol. Whether you realize it or not, you are being yanked around by a yoke of bondage, a yoke of oppression.

SO HOW DO WE HELP PEOPLE IN NEED OF RECOVERY?

Celebrate Recovery is a program designed and originated through Rick Warren and John Baker of Saddleback Church in Lake Forest, California. There are eight Recovery Principles based on the Beatitudes, which are part of the teachings of Jesus known as the Sermon on the Mount found in chapters 5-7 of the gospel of Matthew. These principles are drawn from the Twelve Steps of Celebrate Recovery, which are virtually identical to other Twelve Step programs, but each step is fortified with biblical wisdom. The lesson plans of Celebrate Recovery take twenty-six weeks (half a year), which is a considerable commitment, but many have found this Christian Twelve Step program to be helpful.

The original Twelve Steps of Alcoholics Anonymous, established by Dr. Bob Smith and Bill Wilson in 1935, always have had spiritual roots and made references to God. *These Twelve Steps are consistent and reliable, providing perpetual, positive influence, as demonstrated by the successful sobriety of millions of people in recovery.* They are not the last word in recovery, but they remain an important set of reminders for people.

Bill Wilson has maintained recognition for his contribution to Alcoholics Anonymous. Participants of AA programs frequently identify themselves with a code of fellowship by saying, "I'm a friend of Bill." Wilson states "The Twelve Steps of our AA program are not crammed down anybody's throat. They are not sustained by any human authority. Yet we powerfully unite around them because the truth they contain has saved our lives, has opened the door to a new world... *Alcoholics Anonymous* has no 'musts.' Compliance or non-compliance with any AA principle is a matter of conscience of the individual."[165]

There was wisdom in the establishment of the Twelve Steps so long ago, and there is wisdom in these statements by Bill Wilson. These steps are presented as suggestions. As such, there is freedom to embrace the process or to choose which steps resonate with the person working through recovery. The facilitator of any of the AA meetings is in effect saying to the participant, "The ball is in your court." A person should not be going through the motions of following a series of steps. The freedom to choose folds into the overall motivation of the person recovering. Motivation is paramount. Motivation is the fuel that runs the engine of recovery. During life coaching, the sharpening of goals and the seeking of dreams in a plan for living calls upon motivation for fulfillment in life. Goals and dreams motivate.

The Twelve Steps of Alcoholics Anonymous are totally synonymous with the Twelve Steps of Celebrate Recovery and the Twelve Steps of Narcotics Anonymous. These steps address *addiction*. The strength and validity of these steps has made them a worthy program for recovery.

Most cities in the U.S. provide an online list of community resources for recovery. I was going to include a *Resources* segment at the back of this book, but the need for resources is always a local one, and a list cannot address all communities. Yes, there are multiple international organizations, too many to list. *In most areas, when you want help with recovery, a quick search on someone's phone will reveal many options.* Many services and ministries don't necessarily make it onto community lists.

Here is what I recommend to the people I'm trying to help:

1. *Commit to God*
2. *Seek Resources*
3. *Attend Meetings*

As helpful as the Alcoholics Anonymous/ Cocaine Anonymous/ Narcotics Anonymous meetings are, they represent just a portion of what should be a comprehensive approach to recovery. *Recovery has to be embraced by someone who wants to recover.* Ongoing sobriety and recovery require the help of others. Rehab centers can aid in detox and treatment. A person in recovery should not only attend meetings, but seek counseling, mentoring, coaching, Bible studies, and Christian fellowship.

Intervention helps. The following is an example of a method of recovery that really works:

> Two friends of mine were part of a weekly Bible study as part of Christian Aftercare Ministries for former prisoners. One of them, Dave, was doing well in recovery and had been sober for several months. His health was better. He was thinking and speaking more clearly and had a spring in

his step. He was celebrating his progress. But he
had a relapse. My other friend, Richie, encountered Dave at a park, down on the grass, high and
mumbling. Richie grabbed him by the collar of
his shirt and said, "You can do better than this!"
Richie took him to the Farnum Center where
Dave spent a month in rehab treatment and
continued with an intensive outpatient program
(IOP). Dave returned to the Helping Hands
Outreach Center sober home as a resident, and
once again was on a recovery track. Sad to say,
there was another relapse, and the pattern has
repeated. But Richie's intervention gave Dave
a fighting chance. That fighting chance is what
Christian ministry is about!

Yes, this is the same Richie mentioned in the first chapter.
He continues to encourage the people he knew "back then" to
be in recovery and rebuild their lives. We are all in the same fight!

My friend Mark is another success story. He lived at the
Helping Hands Outreach Center for several months, while
dedicated to his sobriety and working faithfully as a flag person
for traffic at road construction sites. He moved on to a more
independent apartment home, was snapped up by a paving
company for better pay and benefits, and has been sober for
twenty months. He also used to have run-ins with the police,
but recently he was featured on a TV news program for being awarded a set of golf clubs from a police officer who was

impressed with his turn around. One of his new golfing buddies is a former Red Sox baseball player. Mark is another person who is growing in his capacity as a mentor.

There are many people I could feature as success stories. So far, I have invited ten individuals to share their testimonies at 1269 Café, the homeless outreach. These friends of mine were either in prison, were addicted, or were homeless. Most of them have been all three. But now – with God's help, they are sober. They have homes, jobs, restored family connections, better health, and joy in their lives! All of these friends and I are concerned for the next success story, the success story of that person who right now needs to be in recovery.

To do Christian ministry in the inner city is to be *in the recovery business*. Beyond that – praise God! – our LORD is in the recovery business! When Jesus read from the scroll of Isaiah in Luke 4:18, He was describing His mission and ministry, written seven hundred years before He came along:

> The Spirit of the LORD is upon Me,
> Because He has anointed Me
> To preach the gospel to the poor;
> He has sent Me to heal the brokenhearted,
> To proclaim liberty to the captives
> And recovery of sight to the blind,
> To set at liberty those who are oppressed.

Preaching the gospel to the poor is an aid to recovery. Healing the brokenhearted helps with recovery. Proclaiming liberty to the captives leads to recovery. Recovery of sight to the blind *is* recovery. Setting at liberty those who are oppressed is a way of recovery.

Jesus could have gone on to say: "And in order to do these things, The Holy Spirit will establish Christian Aftercare Ministries, Makeover Ministry, Rise Again Outreach, Food for Children, 1269 Café, Harmony Home, Celebrate Recovery, and Helping Hands Outreach Center!" And this is just a partial list of Christian ministries in one city in 'little old New Hampshire.' Each one of these ministries was begun by followers of Jesus Christ. Each one of these ministries helps out in the process of recovery.

Those that struggle with the need for recovery should reach through all of the meetings, resources, and ministries that are offered to *connect with the LORD Himself!* He has the power, the might, the ability to provide you with complete recovery!

Please consider these words from Psalm 94:

> Blessed is the man whom You instruct, O LORD, And teach out of Your law, That You may give him rest from the days of adversity, Until the pit is dug for the wicked. For the LORD will not cast off His people, nor will He forsake His inheritance. But judgment will return to righteousness, and all the upright in heart will follow it. Who will rise up for me against the evildoers? Who will stand up for me against the workers of iniquity? Unless

the LORD had been my help, my soul would soon have settled in silence. If I say, "My foot slips," Your mercy, O LORD, will hold me up. In the multitude of my anxieties within me, Your comforts delight my soul" (Psalm 94:12-19).

Unless the LORD had been my help, I wouldn't have recovered from a broken marriage while still in my twenties. But the LORD *was* my help. My foot slipped, and the LORD held me up. I have been re-married for going on four decades now. The LORD can *Hold You Up!* The Holy Spirit has established ministries and resources around the world. *The LORD is the strongest power source of recovery available to everyone.*

My experiences with prisoners, among the homeless, halfway houses, and struggling people in poor countries have fortified a profound understanding: The spiritual realm of life is not an invisible, minor, inconsequential facet of daily living. Having faith in Jesus Christ is not just sorta, kinda helpful when it comes to recovery, when it comes to rebuilding your life. Faith in Jesus Christ is pivotal, central, momentous, critical, vital, and crucial! *The LORD is the strongest power source for recovery, the rebuilding of lives, and the breaking of yokes available to everyone.*

What is your burden? Are you carrying a yoke that we can't see? What is your recovery need? LORD, this is our prayer – that whatever extent of recovery is needed by each person, that You be instrumental in our recovery – that You be our Recoverer! In Jesus' Name, Amen!

CHAPTER 12

ALL HANDS ON DECK

From the era of sailing ships to the time of modern naval cruisers, the crews on board work, eat, rest, and have private time in shifts. Traveling at sea requires twenty-four hours of vigilance every day, and crewpersons spend so many hours on duty with corresponding down time. When a crisis occurs, such as a violent storm or an enemy attack, the entire crew is alerted. The chief mate or perhaps the second mate, at the captain's order, would yell down an open hatch in the days of sailing vessels or announce through intercom in modern ships, "All hands on deck!" The needs of former prisoners released into the halfway house setting and homeless people in all major cities quietly cries out the existence of a crisis. We need *all hands on deck*.

Christian churches throughout the United States are familiar with the need for assistance in prison. These ministries can always use some expansion, and if an individual or a team senses a calling to do prison ministry, it should be easy enough to

ALL HANDS ON DECK

network through local churches, either joining an existing program or starting a new one. Prison ministry represents a need which is recognized in churches throughout the United States. *However, in the case of halfway houses, there are very few Christian ministries. It represents a void.* Major cities like Manchester, New Hampshire do have resources for those in halfway houses, with local access to drug and alcohol rehabilitation, counseling, medical help and welfare. There are Christian Licensed Alcohol and Drug Abuse Counselors (LADAC's) and Christian mental health counselors available, as well as sufficient churches in the local area within walking distance. The individual who newly arrives at the halfway house has a daunting challenge. He or she has to find out about these resources and where the offices are located. They have to figure out how to obtain the right ID's and where there might be work. During this time, they have to follow the curfew and visitation rules of the house. On top of that, the individual attempts to reconnect with family members under circumstances which frequently involve brokenness.

I have been mentioning so much about the ministries in my local city. It's personal, but what good would Christianity be if it didn't get personal? I'm explaining the circumstances that I and colleagues experience so they can be helpful for you to apply to people in need near you.

The housing unit known as Helping Hands Outreach Center has many residents who are directly released from prison. Helping Hands is their halfway house. Some of the residents at Helping Hands formerly were at the Calumet halfway house. There are also some former residents of Calumet who are unfortunately homeless. Do you notice how frequently we are considering the former prisoner and soon mention the homeless person? It is because their experiences overlap. I try to separate these two topics in order to address them properly, yet they are often both represented in the same single person.

The 1269 Café ministry to the homeless is known in the Manchester community for the many things it offers, like a daily lunch, a food pantry, showers, programs, and Medicated Assisted Treatment (MAT) schedules for opioid addiction. The programs provide Christian encouragement in faith. The people are willing to listen because they respect the fact that they are being fed and helped. I have invited all Helping Hands residents to the Sunday service at 1269 Café, where a series of ten people have given their testimonies over recent months. These people exemplify transformed lives!

A COLLAGE OF RECENT TESTIMONIES GIVEN
DURING SUNDAY SERVICES AT 1269 CAFÉ

Christianity helps people rebuild their lives. My friend Joshua is a faithful attendee of our weekly Bible study. He wrote the below testimony:

> I was brought up in Manchester, New Hampshire, largest town in New England north of Boston. my mother first met my dad at the state prison halfway house in the downtown area in 1988. my dad has always carried anger and hostile mindset stemming from his traumatic childhood. December 1994, when I was five, my mother dozed off at the wheel of her car, struck a tree, and passed away soon after the accident. my dad didn't quite know what to do but press on and keep his two boys from seeing the state foster care system. dad would smack us, close-fist punch us, choke us, throw things at us, he beat us like men. I believe he was a broken young man with a heart filled with pain. in 1996 he met my step mother and her daughter. my step mother was relentless in beating me and making me stand in the corner, or sit on the stairs for hours and days. I whined to myself and day dreamed, wishing my situation was different, that my teachers at school would find out about what was happening and people would rescue me from my home life. during my middle school

years, I was bullied and had few friends. I was quiet and thin and wore clothes that didn't fit me. I sought comfort from my music and video games. in high school I began hanging out with a large group of kids who smoked butts and weed and skipped class every day. I started drinking, huffing aerosol cans, taking pills I had no business taking. if it got me high, I wanted to do it. I was obsessed with smoking weed. it was an escape from reality, I hated who I was. At 16 I started slashing my arms open, burning myself, listening to dark music. I was in a relationship with a girl I treated absolutely terrible. no woman should go through what I put her through. at 18 I started becoming more of a lunatic, I ran around Manchester giving everyone a hard time. eventually I was placed in prison for four years for setting a fire at a local retail store. making prison home for an extended period of time was strangely not hard for me. it became very normal, very quickly. I was deeply depressed, anxious, lonely, confused. I my family and friends rarely contacted me. I read a lot about various religions seeking truth where there was none. I sought love and community in a interracial gang that approached me about joining. I didn't know what I was getting in to. I didn't care about what happened to me anymore. after being placed in a segregated housing unit for threatening an officer's life, my cell mate Joshua, asked me if I knew Jesus. I quickly built walls in resistance. I'll always remember him quoting Matthew 11, "Come unto Me, all of you who are weary and carry heavy burdens, and I will give you rest. Take up My yoke and learn from Me, for I am lowly and humble in heart, and you will find rest for your souls. For My yoke is easy and My burden is light." I understand today that God was inviting me to His table and preparing a place for me even in my unbelief. after parting with my friend Joshua and leaving prison in September 2014 I stumbled across 1269 Café, a ministry on the front lines of the center city homeless and drug epidemic that has left its mark on Manchester for years. I wanted to do something with my time and asked someone if I could help serve coffee and join clean up after closing time. I made many close friends in serving at 1269. outside 1269, I had no home, I was an alcoholic, drug seeking, aimless. but Jesus always speaks a better word. I'd go to these local Bible studies because they had food and coffee. this was my semi-usual routine for months. one cold winter night I was desperate for Jesus to come in to my heart. it was certainly a genuine moment of desperation. I was so tired of chasing the wind. soon later I'd fall in to crystal meth addiction. my dear friends Craig and Mary sent me to Massachusetts to Salvation Army rehabilitation center. there was such a strong desire to know Jesus at this time but I was concerned about everyone else. anger consumed me and I was asked to leave after four months. I was so frustrated with my life, I pushed Jesus far away. I wanted nothing to do with Him anymore. I wandered Springfield for about a week and a local church had mercy on me and bought me food and a bus ticket to Nashua, New Hampshire. one day back in downtown Manchester my friend Mark gave me a leather ESV study Bible. I would carry this thing everywhere I went. In March 2018 I fell back in to crystal meth. I made my home in a food truck and smoked all night, all morning. God's Spirit broke through the grip that drug had on me and I started texting my friend Jackie Scripture verse after Scripture verse as I frantically turned the pages of my Bible in what I now know was intense warfare. on the morning of March 25, I decided to stop completely and I rededicate my heart back to His. Jesus used Harmony Home Ministry in a powerful way to keep me steeped in love, commitment,

ALL HANDS ON DECK

worship, prayer, and just a safe place to hang
out during the day. January, 2020, I went to
the capital of Jordan with a young adults' group
and ministered to broken Muslim men for sev-
en week period. I never imagined I'd be able
to leave the U.S. after being incarcerated in
state prison. today I know God's love is greater
than my past hurts and failures. I receive His
invitation of grace. Jesus is always calling us to
Himself. He is beyond amazing.

WHERE DO YOU COME IN?

Many of you *are* doing ministry among those in need. Praise
God, the many ministries and outreaches of towns and cities around the world have quietly, faithfully, provided food,
shelter, clothing, compassion, and evangelism. What can you
bring? The answer is – Whatever You Have. Whoever You Are.
In the slang, *Bring What You Got!* You don't have to initiate a
Bible study or a recovery ministry when you can come alongside one that already exists. Or you can notice a need and find a
way to fill it. You could start a "socks and underwear" ministry,
or a "shoes and boots" ministry, or a "winter hats and gloves"
ministry. You can help out in a local food pantry or soup kitch-
en, or start one if the need is near you. Visiting folks in halfway
houses doesn't require a theological education. Your being willing to listen is immensely valuable.

Redemption is the culmination of all of the benefits of following the LORD. Redemption is the desire of God's heart for

everyone He has made. Three phrases from Bible verses below affirm amazing insight into the capacity that our LORD God has to rebuild lives and break yokes of oppression:

> We have seen that through faith in Jesus Christ, we are *"redeemed from the hand of the enemy"* (Psalm 107:2). Let's consider this next verse: *"He has delivered us from the power of darkness* and conveyed us into the kingdom of the Son of His love" (Colossians 1 1:13). Notice that deliverance is part of our redemption. These promises in God's Word assure us that we are redeemed from the hand of the enemy and that we have been delivered from the power of darkness!
>
> The power of darkness in this world is real. It has resulted in addictions, divorce, despair, strife, poverty, homelessness, depression, brokenness, warfare, and on and on. There are powers and principalities having their way with people: "For we do not wrestle against flesh and blood, but against principalities, against powers, against the rulers of the darkness of this age, against spiritual hosts of wickedness in the heavenly places (Ephesians 6:12). Yokes of oppression are pushing many around! But consider this message from God about those of us who have faith in Jesus Christ:

"He has made alive together with Him, having forgiven you all trespasses, having wiped out the handwriting of requirements that was against us, which was contrary to us. And He has taken it out of the way, having nailed it to the cross. *Having disarmed principalities and powers*, He made a public spectacle of them, triumphing over them in it" (Colossians 2:13-15). *Principalities and powers are disarmed! We are redeemed from the hand of the enemy and we have been delivered from the power of darkness!*[166]

Understanding the truth of these statements should sink down into our hearts and spirits, and be tamped down into the hearts and spirits of those who struggle.

The LORD is the strongest power source of recovery, rebuilding of lives, and breaking of yokes available to everyone. It takes YOU and other people who know and love the LORD, as part of Christian fellowship, to provide the coaching, mentoring, pastoral counseling, Bible studies and programs, accompanied by encouragement, enlightenment, and inspiration! Halfway house residents, former prisoners, and homeless people around town buckling under their heavy yokes of oppression need YOU! Consider helping them to rebuild their lives and *break every yoke.*

HISTORY TO REFLECT UPON

PRISONERS IN THE OLD TESTAMENT
The earliest person in biblical history referred to as a prisoner is
Joseph, the eleventh son of Jacob. Joseph had been sold as a slave
to Ishmaelites. They in turn sold him to an Egyptian, Potiphar,
who was an officer of Pharaoh and captain of the guard. Joseph
was made overseer of this captain's house. Potiphar's wife lusted
after Joseph, and falsely accused him of attempting to seduce
her, when in fact he had run away from her. Potiphar felt he
had been betrayed and sent Joseph to prison.

> Then Joseph's master took him and put him
> into the prison, a place where the king's pris-
> oners were confined. And he was there in the
> prison. But the LORD was with Joseph and
> showed him mercy, and He gave him favor in
> the sight of the keeper of the prison. And the
> keeper of the prison committed to Joseph's

hand all the prisoners who were in the prison;
whatever they did there, it was his doing
(Genesis 39:20-22).

Amazingly, because the favor of the LORD was upon
Joseph, not only was he put in charge of Potiphar's household,
but he was also put in charge of his fellow prisoners. Joseph was
unjustly imprisoned.

Joseph was to interact with two other prisoners: "It came to
pass after these things that the butler and the baker of the king
of Egypt offended their LORD, the king of Egypt. And Pharaoh
was angry with his two officers, the chief butler and the chief
baker. So he put them in custody in the house of the captain
of the guard, in the prison, the place where Joseph was confined" (Genesis 40:1-3). Joseph accurately interpreted dreams
for these two prisoners, which eventually became a ticket out
of prison for Joseph. The chief butler mentioned Joseph's ability to interpret dreams to the Pharaoh, who had a perplexing
dream of his own. Joseph's interpretation of Pharaoh's dream
was well received. "Then Pharaoh said to Joseph, 'Inasmuch as
God has shown you all this, there is no one as discerning and
wise as you. You shall be over my house, and all my people shall
be ruled according to your word; only in regard to the throne
will I be greater than you.' And Pharaoh said to Joseph, "See,
I have set you over all the land of Egypt" (Genesis 41:39-41).
Joseph was yet again put in charge. This time, he was in a position to help his brothers from the land of Canaan who had
suffered from famine.

This historical account of Joseph demonstrates that the favor of the LORD is evident to others. Joseph was able to overcome being sold into slavery and being unjustly imprisoned. In addition to being an overcomer, he was able to forgive his brothers and bless their lives. Joseph's "halfway house" was the Egyptian Pharaoh's palace. His faith in the LORD sustained him in each setting he found himself. These qualities evident in Joseph could help the current halfway house resident.

Another account of imprisonment is found in Numbers 21:1. "The king of Arad, the Canaanite, who dwelt in the South, heard that Israel was coming on the road to Atharim. Then he fought against Israel and took some of them *prisoners*." These Israelites were prisoners of their enemy, in a circumstance equivalent to being prisoners of war. The justice of such an imprisonment is understandably different from the perspective of one nation versus another. The tide of circumstance, in this case, was changed by the LORD. "So Israel made a vow to the LORD, and said, 'If You will indeed deliver this people into my hand, then I will utterly destroy their cities.' And the LORD listened to the voice of Israel and delivered up the Canaanites, and they utterly destroyed them and their cities" (Numbers 21:2-3). It's good it is to have the LORD on your side!

The experience of being a captive of your enemy has the added weight of hatred, or at the least a sense of scorn, coming from the captors. In an American prison, the prison staff are presumably neutral in the carrying out of their duties. But even in modern times, prisoners are frequently seen almost as an enemy, deserving of punishment, even after their sentence is complete. This stigma is part of the experience of the person in a halfway house.

Samson became a prisoner of the Philistines through the deceit of Delilah, a woman who was not his wife: "Then the Philistines took him and put out his eyes, and brought him down to Gaza. They bound him with bronze fetters, and he became a grinder in the prison" (Judges 16:21).

A pattern or cycle exists throughout the Book of Judges:

- *Sin:* "The Israelites did evil in the eyes of the LORD."
- *War as Judgement:* "The LORD sold them into the hands of X (enemy nation) for X years.
- *Repentance:* But when the Israelites cried out to the LORD…"
- *Deliverance:* "… he raised up for them a deliverer, X (name of judge), who saved them.[167]

Israel was the name given Jacob, an individual who became a nation through his offspring. Israel, as a nation, sometimes reflects the personality of an individual. The historical recORD of Israel in the Bible provides life lessons to be learned through the nation's behavior. Individuals today frequently reflect the cycle of events reflected in the Book of Judges. In the case of prisoners, phase two (*War as Judgement*) becomes *Imprisonment as Judgement*. When a prisoner is released into a halfway house, the best outcome for that individual would reflect the next two phases of this same pattern – *Repentance and Deliverance*. This hope is the heart of Christian ministry.

The Israelite king, Ahab, imprisoned a prophet of God. "Then the king of Israel said, 'Take Micaiah, and return him to Amon the governor of the city and to Joash the king's son; and say, "Thus says the king: 'Put this fellow in prison, and feed him with bread of affliction and water of affliction, until I return in peace" ' " (2 Chronicles 18:25-26). The entire story of Ahab and the prophet Michaiah straddles the books of 2nd Chronicles and 1st Kings. Micaiah was accurately conveying the Word of God as he stated: "Therefore look! The LORD has put a lying spirit in the mouth of these prophets of yours, and the LORD has declared disaster against you" (2 Chronicles 18:22). King Ahab was "shooting the messenger," or at least imprisoning him. Michaiah was a political prisoner.

In the 2nd Book of Kings, there is an account of the fall and captivity of Jerusalem. In the year 597 BC, Jehoiachin surrendered to the Neo-Babylonian monarch Nebuchadnezzar.[168] "Then Jehoiachin king of Judah, his mother, his servants, his princes, and his officers went out to the king of Babylon; and the king of Babylon, in the eighth year of his reign, took him *prisoner*" (2 Kings 24:12). This was beyond being an enemy captive. It was the conquering of a nation. Jerusalem was laid under terrible siege and fell in 586 BC after frightful famine. The city was burned and the inhabitants deported or slain. Jeremiah records, "in the eighteenth year of Nebuchadnezzar he carried away captive from Jerusalem eight hundred and thirty-two persons" (Jeremiah 52:29). Jehoiachin was released from prison after thirty-seven years by Nebudchadnezzar II's successor, Evil-Merodach

(Amel-Marduk, Akkadian, "man of Marduk"), 562-560 BC. The biblical account of this release is poignant: "So Jehoiachin changed from his prison garments, and he ate bread regularly before the king all the days of his life. And as for his provisions, there was a regular ration given him by the king, a portion for each day, all the days of his life" (2 Kings 25:29-30). These provisions were acts of kindness toward a fallen enemy. Shouldn't such kindness be extended to people who have committed crimes, and need to begin again?

The biblical character Job is famous for being troubled in a big way. At one point he bemoans these troubles, and wishes he was dead: "why was I not hidden like a stillborn child, like infants who never saw light? There the wicked cease from troubling, and there the weary are at rest. There the *prisoners* rest together; they do not hear the voice of the oppressor" (Job 3:16-18). In his suffering, Job demonstrates sympathy and compassion for the prisoner. He identifies with their need for rest and their need to be spared from the taunting of those who oppress them. The LORD, with His characteristic of loving-kindness, or *hesed*, has a heart for the oppressed. The LORD desires that the oppressed be set free: "Is this not the fast that I have chosen: To loose the bonds of wickedness, To undo the heavy burdens, To let the *oppressed* go free, And that you break every yoke?" (Isaiah 58:6). The psalmist also emphasizes: "The LORD also will be a refuge for the *oppressed*, A refuge in times of trouble" (Psalm 9:9). And this compassion is shared by Job, who is described this way: "that man was blameless and upright, and one who feared God and shunned evil"

(Job 1:1). This compassion is meant to be shared by all of the followers of Jesus Christ!

In the Book of Isaiah, the following judgement is pronounced:

> What will you do in the day of punishment, and in the desolation which will come from afar? To whom will you flee for help? And where will you leave your glory? Without Me they shall bow down among the *prisoners*, and they shall fall among the slain (Isaiah 10:3-4a).

Unger's New Bible Handbook describes it this way, "Captivity was imminent for the ruthless ruling class in Samaria who heartlessly exploited their subjects." *Harper's Bible Commentary* describes the passage as "a lengthy attack on corrupt Judean judges who leave the people without any recourse to justice."[169] The LORD has compassion for the prisoner, and counts him among the oppressed, yet the LORD acknowledges that some are deserving of the punishment of prison.

The LORD condemns Lucifer in another series of judgement pronouncements in Isaiah. "Those who see you will gaze at you, and consider you, saying: 'Is this the man who made the earth tremble, who shook kingdoms, who made the world as a wilderness and destroyed its cities, who did not open the house of his *prisoners*?' (Isaiah 14:16-17). Lucifer does *not* have compassion upon the prisoner. This stands in contrast to the announcement of Jesus' ministry and mission, described in a reading from the scroll of Isaiah, recorded in Luke

4:18-19. "The Spirit of the LORD GOD is upon Me, because the LORD has anointed Me to preach good tidings to the poor; He has sent Me to heal the brokenhearted, to proclaim liberty to the captives, and the opening of the prison to *those who are bound*" (Isaiah 61:1). This Isaiah passage is so prominent that Jesus read it directly from the scroll and made a powerful statement: "Today this Scripture is fulfilled in your hearing" (Luke 4:21). Jesus was revealing Himself as the Messiah.

The wording is different in Luke 4:18 and Isaiah 61:1. Where the New testament reads "recovery of sight to the blind, to set at liberty those who are oppressed" the original Old Testament verse reads "the opening of the prison to those who are bound." We see these nuances between different Bible translations today, but something important is being expressed. *The meaning of these passage is identical.* Harper's *Bible Commentary* makes a significant observation regarding the terminology of this Isaiah passage, specifically the phrase "To proclaim liberty to the captives, and the opening of the prison to *those who are bound*" (latter portion of Is 61:1). Here is that observation: "As in 42:7 and 49:9, those for whom salvation has not yet occurred are called prisoners." *According to this view, the LORD considers those who are unsaved to be prisoners!* The two verses referred to read as follows: "To open blind eyes, to bring out prisoners from the prison, those who sit in darkness from the prison house" (Isaiah 42:7); and "That You may say to the prisoners, 'Go forth,' to those who are in darkness, 'Show yourselves.' "They shall feed along the roads, and their pastures shall be on all desolate heights" (Isaiah 49:9). These prisoners are described as having "blind eyes" and being "in darkness." These descriptions are a metaphor for the unsaved! This provides new insight into our motivation for proclaiming liberty to the captives," and "the opening of the prison to those who are bound"! The homeless and those who have been in prison, as well as all those who don't believe in the LORD – are captive, bound, prisoners!

In 588-587 BC, while Jerusalem is under siege, Zedekiah king of Judah imprisoned Jeremiah the prophet "for prophesying, first, that Yahweh will deliver Jerusalem to Nebuchadnezzar; second, that Zedekiah will not escape but will be given into the hand of the king of Babylon, brought before him, and taken to Babylon, where he will remain until Yahweh 'visits' him; and third, that fighting against the Babylonians will not be successful." At first, Jeremiah was put into prison: "For then the king of Babylon's army besieged Jerusalem, and Jeremiah the prophet was shut up in the court of the prison, which was in the king of Judah's house" (Jeremiah 32:2). Later, Jeremiah suffered worse consequences: "So they took Jeremiah and cast him into the dungeon of Malchiah the king's son, which was in the court of the prison, and they let Jeremiah down with ropes. And in the dungeon, there was no water, but mire. So Jeremiah sank in the mire" (Jeremiah 38:6). The American Heritage Desk Dictionary defines *mire* as: (1) An area of wet, soggy, and muddy ground; a bog. (2) Deep, slimy soil or mud.[170] Jeremiah was correct in his prophesies. He was imprisoned for being the bearer of bad news. Yet he was effectively conveying the Word of God!

Jeremiah was in effect a political prisoner, as was Micaiah, mentioned earlier. Political prisoners are subject to shifting control of power. Elements of politics and power struggle in the current state of drug laws in the United States factor into the complicated struggle prisoners and former prisoners face, as they frequently feel "stuck in the mire."

After the fall of Jerusalem, from 588 to 586 BC, as many were taken in exile, the captain of the guard offered the choice to Jeremiah whether to be exiled in Babylon or remain in Palestine, saying, "And now look, I free you this day from the chains that were on your hand" (Jeremiah 40:4a). Jeremiah was permitted to continue ministering to the Jews in Palestine. But it did not go well for the king who had imprisoned him "Then the king of Babylon killed the sons of Zedekiah before his eyes. And he killed all the princes of Judah in Riblah. He also put out the eyes of Zedekiah; and the king of Babylon bound him in bronze fetters, took him to Babylon, and put him in prison till the day of his death" (Jeremiah 52:10-11).

The prophet Daniel and others were taken captive by Nebuchadnezzar in 605 B.C., who "took only the most noble and promising. Daniel was of royal birth, highly gifted and showed great promise. His moral faith and spiritual courage were proved in his decision for godly separation from the defilement of Babylon."[171] Daniel was not strictly a prisoner, but a captive living in exile. Daniel outlived Nebuchadnezzar and his successor Belshazzar, and was respected by King Darius, who appointed Daniel as one of three governors. "Then this Daniel distinguished himself above the governors and satraps, because an excellent spirit was in him; and the king gave thought to setting him over the whole realm" (Daniel 6:3). This led to jealousy by the other leaders. "He is now in his eighties, and his enemies still cannot fault him. They can only attack him through his religion. Daniel could have stopped praying for a month, or he could have prayed in secret. But he is no more ready to compromise now than he was as a boy. So his enemies have him. The king's hands are tied by his own decree, but God's hand is not."[172] Daniel had been a captive in exile most of his life, and he was to be imprisoned in a unique prison, a den of lions. "So the king gave the command, and they brought Daniel and cast him into the den of lions. But the king spoke, saying to Daniel, 'Your God, whom you serve continually, He will deliver you' " (Daniel 6:16). Zach Sewell provides this perspective, "When Daniel entered the lion's den, most people counted him out. Whether they liked Daniel or hated him, most people probably thought he would die in there. Daniel, however, surprised them by emerging from the lion's den unharmed. He survived because he trusted God (Daniel 6:23)."[173] Sewell adds insight and inspiration to the account of Daniel as he writes:

> When you entered prison, people may have counted you out. People may not expect much from you once you leave prison. But with God's help, you can leave prison and make a positive impact on the world around you – even if nobody expects you to. That's what Daniel did

(Daniel 6:25-28). When he climbed out of the lions' den, he fought against corruption and evil. What do you trust God will help you do when you leave prison?

These thoughts and this rhetorical question provide the kind of encouragement and inspiration that is so important in the halfway house setting. In addition to the question "What do you trust God will help you do when you leave prison?" I add "What do you trust God will help you do for those that recently got out of prison and need a hand up?

Old Testament books tell stories of real people. By reading the accounts of those in captivity and prison, we recognize that the denial of freedom is a universal timeless reality. "Stand fast therefore in the liberty by which Christ has made us free, and do not be entangled again with a *yoke of bondage*" (Galatians 5:1).

PRISONERS IN THE NEW TESTAMENT

The imprisonment of John the Baptist is mentioned early in the Gospels: "Now when Jesus heard that John had been put in prison, He departed to Galilee" (Mathew 4:12), and the parallel account: "Now after John was put in prison, Jesus came to Galilee, preaching the gospel of the kingdom of God" (Mark 1:14). John's arrest is explained in the gospel of Mark.

For Herod himself had sent and laid hold of John and bound him in prison for the sake of Herodias, his brother Philip's wife; for he had

married her. Because John had said to Herod, "It
is not lawful for you to have your brother's wife."
Therefore, Herodias held it against him and wanted to kill him, but she could not; for Herod feared
John, knowing that he was a just and holy man,
and he protected him (Mark 6:17-20).

Harper's Bible Commentary speaks of the narrative in the
Gospel of Mark describing the passion and death of John the
Baptist: "It illustrates the risk of a prophetic life-style that con-
fronts brutal power and prefigures the subsequent execution
and arrest of Jesus."[174]

In a moment of weakness and doubt, John the
Baptist waivers. "And John, calling two of his disciples
to him, sent them to Jesus, saying, 'Are You the Coming One,
or do we look for another?' When the men had come to Him,
they said, "John the Baptist has sent us to You, saying, 'Are You
the Coming One, or do we look for another?'" (Luke 7:19-20).
Sewell writes, "Tough questions for God are natural even for
people who have a deep faith, like John did. In prison, we can
doubt things we were once certain of. Like John, we may want
to ask God, 'Are you really who I think you are?' It is better to
ask tough questions of God than to abandon your faith altogether."[175] John's uncertainty reveals some of the nature of imprisonment. There is not only confinement, but a stigma about
who you are, a cloud of disregard or of contempt. John was
second-guessing. A sense of confidence in oneself is difficult
to maintain in a prison setting. And those who have just come

from that experience have to shake themselves loose from the cloud or stigma which accompanies them.

John underwent capital punishment in the form of beheading at the whim of an angry woman and her daughter. This was murder, not justice. Most of the imprisonments recorded throughout the Bible are an injustice! But the LORD has a heart of compassion for all prisoners, whether or not the sentencing is fair.

Jesus warned the disciples that they would be imprisoned on His behalf: "they will lay their hands on you and persecute you, delivering you up to the synagogues and prisons. You will be brought before kings and rulers for My name's sake (Luke 21:12). Peter expressed his willingness to suffer for the LORD on another occasion. "LORD, I am ready to go with You, both to prison and to death" (Luke 22:33). Unfortunately, this was stated the same night Peter denied the LORD three times. Ultimately, with the power of the Holy Spirit, Peter was able to follow through with his vow.

Jesus arrest, suffering, and death on the cross is the centerpiece of history. His is the grand finale of prison accounts, the ultimate proclamation of liberty for the captives (Luke 4:18), the ultimate opening of the prison to those who are bound (Isaiah 61:1)! When Jesus died, He died a prisoner. The LORD understands what it is like to be a prisoner. His treatment was not lenient. "Then the detachment of troops and the captain and the officers of the Jews arrested Jesus and bound Him" (John 18:12). And not long afterward, "Now the men who held Jesus mocked Him and beat Him. And having blindfolded Him, they struck

Him on the face and asked Him, saying, 'Prophesy! Who is the one who struck You?' And many other things they blasphemously spoke against Him" (Luke 22:63-65). After Jesus was turned over to Pontius Pilate, the governor gave the crowd an option: "Now at the feast the governor was accustomed to releasing to the multitude one prisoner whom they wished. And at that time they had a notorious prisoner called Barabbas (Matthew 27:15-16). The crowd demanded Barabbas.

> So Pilate, wanting to gratify the crowd, released Barabbas to them; and he delivered Jesus, after he had scourged Him, to be crucified. Then the soldiers led Him away into the hall called Praetorium, and they called together the whole garrison. And they clothed Him with purple; and they twisted a crown of thorns, put it on His head, and began to salute Him, "Hail, King of the Jews!" Then they struck Him on the head with a reed and spat on Him; and bowing the knee, they worshiped Him. And when they had mocked Him, they took the purple off Him, put His own clothes on Him, and led Him out to crucify Him (Mark 15:15-20).

Portions of Scripture are quoted here in order to emphasize the rough treatment that Jesus endured. His "incarceration" was not for a period of years, but the punishment and pain inflicted upon Him was fatal.

Consider the two who were crucified with Jesus:

> Then one of the criminals who were hanged
> blasphemed Him, saying, "If You are the
> Christ, save Yourself and us." But the other,
> answering, rebuked him, saying, "Do you not
> even fear God, seeing you are under the same
> condemnation? And we indeed justly, for we
> receive the due reward of our deeds; but this
> Man has done nothing wrong." Then he said
> to Jesus, "LORD, remember me when You
> come into Your kingdom." And Jesus said to
> him, "Assuredly, I say to you, today you will be
> with Me in Paradise." (Luke 23: 39-43).

This visual of two prisoners disagreeing on either side of
Jesus is an amazing historical metaphor. They each represent
opposing views of the personhood of Jesus. They represent the
entirety of mankind. Charles Dickens famously wrote *A Tale
of Two Cities*, and this event is a tale of two prisoners. They
represent rejection and acceptance of the LORD. Every true
believer has symbolically asked, "LORD, remember me when
You come into Your kingdom"!

Then the moment of salvation took place. "Now it was
about the sixth hour, and there was darkness over all the earth
until the ninth hour. Then the sun was darkened, and the veil
of the temple was torn in two. And when Jesus had cried out
with a loud voice, He said, 'Father,

"into Your hands I commit My spirit." ' Having said this, He breathed His last" (Luke 23: 44-46).

Even in death, Jesus was put under guard. "Pilate said to them, 'You have a guard; go your way, make it as secure as you know how.' So they went and made the tomb secure, sealing the stone and setting the guard" (Matthew 27:65-66).

But the tomb could not hold Him. Jesus was resurrected and comforted the disciples, "to whom He also presented Himself alive after His suffering by many infallible proofs, being seen by them during forty days and speaking of the things pertaining to the kingdom of God" (Acts 1:3). And while the disciples watched, "He was taken up, and a cloud received Him out of their sight" (Acts 1:9). Ephesians 4:8 refers to this ascension: "When He ascended on high, He led captivity captive, and gave gifts to men." This is a reference to a prophecy in Psalm 68:18, which Jesus fulfilled and actualized. *The captivity of the world system was itself captured, beaten, and conquered!* Colossians 2:15 puts it this way: "Having disarmed principalities and powers, He made a public spectacle of them, triumphing over them in it." Jesus has triumphed, enabling freedom for those who have been captives: "If you abide in My word, you are My disciples indeed. And you shall know the truth, and the truth shall make you free" (John 8: 31-32).

This concept of freedom is seen in both the Gospels and Epistles of the New Testament:

> Therefore, if the Son makes you free, you shall
> be free indeed. (John 8:36)

But now having been set free from sin, and having become slaves of God, you have your fruit to holiness, and the end, everlasting life. (Romans 6:22)

For the law of the Spirit of life in Christ Jesus has made me free from the law of sin and death. (Romans 8:2)

For the creation was subjected to futility, not willingly, but because of Him who subjected it in hope; because the creation itself also will be delivered from the bondage of corruption into the glorious liberty of the children of God. (Romans 8:20-21)

Now the LORD is the Spirit; and where the Spirit of the LORD is, there is liberty. (2 Corinthians 3:17)

Stand fast therefore in the liberty by which Christ has made us free, and do not be entangled again with a yoke of bondage. (Galatians 5:1)

For this is the will of God, that by doing good you may put to silence the ignorance of foolish men – as free, yet not using liberty as a cloak for vice, but as bondservants of God. (1 Peter 2:15-16)

This freedom is a concept and a reality worth hanging onto for those in halfway houses, the homeless, those who want to help them, and everyone who would like to know and love the LORD! The followers of Jesus were persecuted as He had predicted: "they will lay their hands on you and persecute you, delivering you up to the synagogues and prisons. You will be brought before kings and rulers for My name's sake" (Luke 21:12). As early as the fifth chapter of the Book of Acts, the high priest and some Sadducees: "laid their hands on the apostles and put them in the common prison. But at night an angel of the LORD opened the prison doors and brought them out" (Acts 5:18-19). Another angelic intervention involving incarceration is recorded later in Acts:

> Now about that time Herod the king stretched out his hand to harass some from the church. Then he killed James the brother of John with the sword. And because he saw that it pleased the Jews, he proceeded further to seize Peter also. Now it was during the Days of Unleavened Bread. So when he had arrested him, he put him in prison, and delivered him to four squads of soldiers to keep him, intending to bring him before the people after Passover. (Acts 12:1-4)

Peter was saved miraculously by an angel, complete with chains falling off his hands (Acts 12:7).

Before Saul of Tarsus was dramatically converted to Christianity and became an apostle and writer of epistles which became Scripture, he was a persecutor of Christians, indeed, an *imprisoner*. "At that time a great persecution arose against the church which was at Jerusalem; and they were all scattered throughout the regions of Judea and Samaria, except the apostles. And devout men carried Stephen to his burial, and made great lamentation over him. As for Saul, he made havoc of the church, entering every house, and dragging off men and women, committing them to prison" (Acts 8:1-3).

Saul of Tarsus was renamed Paul, and he was imprisoned with Silas. "Then the multitude rose up together against them; and the magistrates tore off their clothes and commanded them to be beaten with rods. And when they had laid many stripes on them, they threw them into prison, commanding the jailer to keep them securely. Having received such a charge, he put them into the inner prison and fastened their feet in the stocks" (Acts 16:22-24). The incarcerations of the apostles and early Christians were frequently characterized by additional brutality. They were not only imprisoned, but often beaten as well. Paul and Silas's prison term was disrupted miraculously, just as Peter's was.

> But at midnight Paul and Silas were praying and singing hymns to God, and the prisoners were listening to them. Suddenly there was a great earthquake, so that the foundations of the prison were shaken; and immediately all the doors were opened and everyone's chains were loosed.

And the keeper of the prison, awaking from sleep and seeing the prison doors open, supposing the prisoners had fled, drew his sword and was about to kill himself. But Paul called with a loud voice, saying, "Do yourself no harm, for we are all here." Then he called for a light, ran in, and fell down trembling before Paul and Silas. And he brought them out and said, "Sirs, what must I do to be saved? (Acts 16:25-30)

There was an opportunity in this account for the salvation of the keeper of the prison and his entire household. Paul and Silas were exemplary in their concern for the jailer. And an amazing phenomenon is demonstrated: Paul and Silas are entirely at peace before and after the earthquake! They are experiencing the freedom provided by the LORD to the point where they are set free even while imprisoned! This is the extent of freedom which would be insightful and fulfilling for those who have been incarcerated.

Paul was imprisoned several times in accounts seen in Acts, and he went on to write letters or epistles from prison. The "prison epistles" are Ephesians, Colossians, Philippians, and Philemon. There are varying opinions of the possible locations of the writing of these letters:

Where was Paul when he wrote the prison epistles? Three places have been suggested. The earliest is a proposed imprisonment of Paul in

Ephesus, during his third mission, between
A.D. 52 and 55. The next possibility would
be Paul's two-year imprisonment in Caesarea,
A.D. 57 to 59. Finally, Paul's first Roman imprisonment has long served as the "traditional"
setting for the letters (A.D. 60-62).[176]

Paul often mentions being accompanied by other Christian
brothers and sisters as fellow prisoners. "Greet *Andronicus* and
Junia, my countrymen and my fellow prisoners, who are of note
among the apostles, who also were in Christ before me" (Romans
16:7); "*Aristarchus* my fellow prisoner greets you" (Colossians
4:10); *Epaphras,* my fellow prisoner in Christ Jesus, greets you"
(Philemon 1:23). These named prisoners receive honorable mention in the scriptures, and they are the pioneers of so many who
would follow in the early Church and ever since. Paul referred to
himself as the prisoner of the LORD (Ephesians 4:1); prisoner
of Christ Jesus (Ephesians 3:1; Philemon 1:1); and a prisoner in
Christ Jesus (Philemon 1:23).

It is overwhelmingly clear that followers of God have frequently experienced imprisonment. We have these prison accounts because "Holy men of God spoke as they were moved
by the Holy Spirit" (2 Peter 1:21b). But could these "holy men
of God" relate to me, if I've been in prison or did jail time? The
answer is 'of course they could!' The more meaningful question is, *can you relate to them?* The advantage of having the
books of the Bible gathered into one single volume is that we
can read about the lives lived and gain perspective from the

circumstances that others had to go through. The stories of these people are there so we can learn from them.

Jesus can relate to imprisonment. Jesus can relate to suffering. He was arrested and suffered to set you free! Jesus said, "If you abide in My word, you are my disciples indeed. And you shall know the truth, and the truth shall make you free" (John 8:31). Paul considered himself a prisoner of Christ Jesus, a prisoner of the LORD. In other words, he wanted to be held captive to God's way of living. "You have dealt well with Your servant, O LORD, according to Your word. Teach me good judgement and knowledge, for I believe Your commandments. Before I was afflicted, I went astray, but now I keep Your word. You are good, and do good; teach me Your statutes" (Psalm 119:65-68). Join with me, brothers and sisters, in crying out to God, *LORD, strengthen our compassion for those that struggle and help us to break every yoke!*

ACKNOWLEDGEMENTS

Foremost, Thank You LORD, for Your powerful redemptive influence in my life. Gratitude is extended to the following people for the spiritual journey which led to the writing of this book: my parents, Ed and Connie, who supported my studying the Bible outside of the Catholic Church; Dan Lacorazza, who let me tag along and ask questions; my wife Yvonne, who joined me in faithful church and ministry involvement and booked flights when I wondered whether it was possible to go on mission trips; Roland Westervelt, who helped me to calm down on doctrinal matters and baptized our kids; Sam Schreiner, who trusted my connecting with the administrative leadership of the broader church; Mark Swiger, who has inspired and mentored me, a man close to God; Delores Winder, who testified to the miraculous healing power of God; the professors of Gordon-Conwell Theological Seminary at the Center for Urban Ministerial Education, especially Dr. Jim Critchlow, Dr. Eldin Villafane, Dr. Carol

Kaminski, and Drs. Aida and Bill Spencer, who not only published a journal article of mine, but established a ministry in Haiti which I was part of for twelve years; Joseph Delva, Gama Belizaire, Marlane Codair, Eddie Olmstead, Taylor Camerer, Ray Alercia, and Kristi Hunter of that Haiti ministry (Doorway to Peace); Dr. Effie Sidiropoulou, who trained and guided me as a chaplain intern; Jock Dyer, who invited me to do prison ministry with The Authentic Christian Man program at the New Hampshire State Prison for Men in Concord, dear to me, which lasted for fifteen years and led to halfway house involvement; Pastor Al Berja, who invited me to five countries in Asia so that I could experience an overpowering presence of the Holy Spirit, especially in Hong Kong and the Philippines; Dr. Victoria and Andy Schmelzer of Fishers of Men Medical Ministries, for helping me to experience evangelism in Ghana, Africa; Craig and Mary Chevalier, the founders of 1269 Café outreach to the homeless, for trusting and supporting me in speaking, preaching, and teaching for several years; Rinehart Bonnke, the most dynamic speaker I have ever witnessed, who prayed for me along with several others; Vinson Synan, the former dean of Regent University, who I encountered miraculously and who inspired me through his writings regarding the Holiness Movement and Pentecostalism; my professors at Regent University, especially Dr. James Flynn, a living model of encouragement, Dr. Joseph Umidi, who modeled and molded transformational life coaching, and my advisor Dr. Mark

Jumper; my cohorts of the Doctor of Ministry program, especially Samuel Koshy, Kim Stout Jessie, Susan Marie, and Rich Denning, who cheered on my academic progress and ongoing ministry; Pastor Ken Glasier, of my "sending" church, which prayed for my ministry involvements in the city; Owen Carey and John Rivera, the two best preachers in Manchester (even though it's not a contest); my friend and brother Pastor Malcolm Widness, who shares a passion for those struggling; Christian Aftercare Ministries faithful witnesses and servants Paul Roussel and Mike Grady, who bring Bible Studies, encouragement, and evangelism to the local jail and prison, and who let me share their clothing giveaway storage room as my chaplain office; Larry Nice, Helping Hands Outreach Center director and my dissertation field mentor who asked me to serve as chaplain of Helping Hands, the transition home with thirty-five beds, together with board of directors members Dana Teufel, who was with me on one of the Haiti trips, Steve Mitchell, who also served with me on the prison ministry team, and Guy Torgersen, the licensed alcohol and drug counselor who also was on one of the Haiti mission trips, served on the prison ministry team, and who joins with me as part of the worship team at 1269 Café (including the talented guitarist/singer Jack Bailey) while I pound away on the drums; drumming/leadership mentor Jim Buckley; friends I've drummed with, Gary Covitz, Ralph Ciano, Fran Foley, Kevin Shanley, Jim Hager, Jill McCutcheon, Artie Shannon, Steve Wolpe, John 'Choppa' Driscoll, Bill MacDonald,

Charlie Boncore, Chooch Huzz (sorry if you are left out - so many to mention); my bass guitar accompanist and motorcycle buddy Lloyd Wagoner; my editor Renee Crawford, who was spiritually supportive and had great suggestions; life-long friends Bob Constantine, Freddie Fallie, Harry Young, John Petrillo, Dennis Walsh, and Rick Roda, who suggested that the book be one "that our sons would read."

BIBLIOGRAPHY

Alexander, David, and Alexander, Pat, editors, *Eerdmans' Handbook to the Bible*, William B. Eerdmans Publishing Co., Grand rapids, MI, 1976.

Allen, Francis A., *Criminal Justice, Legal Values, and the Rehabilitative Ideal*, from Jeffrie G. Murphy, editor, *Punishment and Rehabilitation*, Belmont, California, Wadsworth Publishing Company, 1985.

Anonymous, *Office of Justice Programs – U. S. Department of Justice; Justice Department Announces Grants Under Second Chance Act Prisoner Reentry Initiative*, Mental Health Weekly Digest; Atlanta, 19 Oct 2009.

Arnold, Bill T., and Beyer, Bryan E., *Encountering the Old Testament: A Christian Survey*, Baker Books, Grand Rapids, MI, 1999.

Batterson, Mark, *The Circle Maker: Praying Dreams Around Your Biggest Dreams and Greatest Fears*, Zondervan, Grand Rapids, MI, 2011.

Bonczar, T., *Prevalence of Imprisonment in the U.S. Population, 1974-2001.* Washington, D.C.: Bureau of Justice Statistics, 2003.

Booth, Demico, *Getting Out & Staying Out: A Black Man's Guide to Success After Prison,* Memphis, TN, Full Surface Publishing, 2012.

Bovan, Richard, *10 Rules for Making it in Society After Doing Time: The Dedicated Ex-Prisoner's Guide to Life and Success on the Outside,* Memphis, TN, Full Surface Publishing, 2009.

Bright, Laurie C., and Graham, Mary G., Faith-Based Programs Give facilities a Helping Hand, *Corrections Today,* Lanham Vol. 69, Iss. 5, (Oct. 2007).

Britannica Academic, s.v. "Halfway house," accessed January 8, 2017, http://0-academic.eb.com.library.regent.edu/levels/collegiate/article/603888

Brown, Raymond, *The Message of Hebrews (The Bible Speaks Today* series), with John R.W. Stott, series editor, IVP Academic, 1984.

Bruce, F. F., *The Epistle to the Hebrews (New International Commentary on the New Testament),* Eerdmans, 1997.

Bruce, F. F., *New Testament History,* Doubleday, 1980.

Buchan, Jim, *Apostolic Evangelism,* Firewind, Mansfield, PA, 2001.

Bultmann, Eleos R., *Theological dictionary of the New Testament,* vol 2. Kittel G, ed. Grand Rapids: Eerdmans, 1982).

Carson, E. A., and Sabol, W. J., *Prisoners in 2011*. Washington, D.C., Bureau of Justice Statistics; Mauer, M., and King, R. (2007). *A 25-Year Quagmire: The War on Drugs and its Impact on American Society.* Washington, D.C.: The Sentencing Project, 2012.

Carson, E. A., and Golinelli, D., *Prisoners in 2012*. Washington, D.C.: Bureau of Justice Statistics, 2013.

Carter, Jimmy, *Faith: A Journey for All*, Simon and Schuster, New York, 2018.

Cavanagh, Susan, Adopt 1, *Edmunton Journal*, Edmunton, Alberta, Canada, 17 May 2014: F.14.

Cei, Louis B., Faith-Based Programs are Low-Cost Ways to Reduce Recidivism, *Corrections Today*; Lanham Vol. 72, Iss. 4, (Aug 2010).

Coleman, Robert E., *The Master Plan of Evangelism*, Fleming H. Revell Co., Grand Rapids, MI, 1993.

Collins, Gary R., *Christian Coaching*, Colorado Springs, CO, NavPress, 2009.

Colman, Andrew M., "halfway house." In *A Dictionary of Psychology*: Oxford University Press, 2015.

Colsen, Chuck, with Morse, Ann, *My Final Word: Holding Tight to the Issues that Matter Most*, Zondervan, Grand Rapids, MI, 2017.

Colson, Charles, with Vaughn, Ellen Santilli, *The Body: Being Light in Darkness*, Dallas, TX, Word Publishing, 1992.

Costanza, S. E., Cox, Stephen M., Kilburn, John C., The Impact of Halfway Houses on Parole Success and Recidivism, *Journal of Sociological Research*, ISSN 1948-5468, 2015, Vol. 6, No. 2.

Crabb, Larry, *Becoming a True Spiritual Community: A Profound Vision of What the Church Can Be*, Nashville, TN, Thomas Nelson, 1999.

Creswell, Jane, *Christ-Centered Coaching: 7 Benefits for Ministry*, Chalice Press, St. Louis, MO, 2006.

Davidson, J., (2016). *Report: Halfway house issues mean high-risk offenders could be released too soon.* Washington: WP Company LLC d/b/a The Washington Post. Retrieved from: http://0-search.proquest.com.library.regent.edu/docview/1841309707?accountid=13479

Dennison, Jack, *City Reaching – On the Road to Community Transformation*, William Carey Library, Pasadena, CA, 1999.

DeRosia, Victoria R., *Living Inside Prison Walls: Adjustment Behavior*, Westport, CT, Praeger Publishers, 1998.

DeSilva, David, *Perseverance in Gratitude: A Socio-Rhetorical Commentary on the Epistle to the Hebrews*, Eerdmans, 2000.

Deurzen, Emmy van and Hanaway, Monica, editors, *Existential Perspectives on Coaching*, Palgrave MacMillan, Hampshire, England, 2012.

Dever, Mark E., *The Gospel and personal Evangelism*, Crossway Books, Wheaton, IL, 2007.

Draper, James, *Hebrews, The Life That Pleases God,* Heartspring Media, 1999.

Evans, Tony, *Discover Your Destiny: Let God Use You Like He Made You,* Harvest House, Eugene, OR, 2013.

Faraonu, Julian, Divine Mercy in the Holy Bible, *Romanian Journal of Artistic Creativity;* Woodside, Vol. 4, Iss. 3, (Autumn 2016).

Feeley, Paul, *President praises Safe Station, calls it 'really quite incredible.'* New Hampshire Union Leader, March 19, 2018.

Ferm, Dr. Robert O., edited by Phillips, Dr. Tom, *The Power of Cooperative Evangelism,* EMIS (Evangelism and Missions Information Service), Wheaton, IL, 2002.

Fike, Doug; Stoltzfus, Tony; Eichman, D. Lyn, *Lifeforming Leadership Coaching, Life Focus Track,* Regent University Bookstore, Virginia Beach, 2008.

Fisher, Mark P., www.samekindofdifferentasmefoundation.org/blog/2018/2/24/7(practical-ways-we-can-help-someone-experiencing-homelessness?)

Forer, Lois G., *A Rage to Punish,* New York, NY, W. W. Norton & Company, 1994.

Gibbons, J. J., & Katzenbach, N.dB, Confronting confinement: A report of the Commission on Safety and Abuse in America's Prisons. Washington, D.C.: Vera Institute of Justice, 2006.

Goleman, Daniel; Boyzatzis, Richard; McKee, Annie, *Primal Leadership: Unleashing the Power of Emotional Intelligence,* Harvard Business School Press, Boston, MA, 2013.

Golomb, Sylvia L., and Kocsis, Andrea, *The Halfway House: On the Road to Independence,* Brunner/ Mazel, Inc., New York, 1988.

Hammond, Kim, and Cronshaw, Darren, *Sentness: Six Postures of Missional Christians,* Downer Grove, IL, InterVarsity Press, 2014.

Harris, Antipas L., *Holy Spirit, Holy Living: Toward a Practical Theology of Holiness for Twenty-First Century Churches,* Eugene, Oregon, Wipf & Stock, 2013.

Hayward, Mark, *Homeless tents demolished Camps in the crosshairs 1 homeless enclave bulldozed, 2 others eyed,* Manchester Union Leader, New Hampshire Sunday News, April 8th, Vol. 72, No. 27, front page.

Henry, Matthew, *Matthew Henry's Concise Commentary on the Whole Bible,* Thomas Nelson, 2003.

Holladay, William L., *A Concise Hebrew and Aramaic Lexicon of the Old Testament (English, Hebrew and Aramaic Edition),* Eerdmans, 1972.

http://biblehub.com/commentaries/gsb/hebrews/13.htm

http://biblehub.com/commentaries/mhc.isaiah/58.htm

http://biblehub.com/commentaries/pulpit/hebrews/13.htm

http://www.gordonconwell.edu/boston/Meet-Our-Staff.cfm

https://www.mih4u.org/recovery/ Community Compass Resources for Greater Manchester, NH.

https://www.nh.gov/nhdoc/divisions/community/calument.html

https://www.sentencingproject.org/criminal-justice-facts/

Ironside, H.A., *The Prophet Isaiah*, Loizeaux Brothers, 1952.

Jennings, F.C., *Studies in Isaiah*, Neptune, NJ: Loizeaux Brothers, 1966.

Johnson, Byron R., *More God, Less Crime: Why Faith Matters and How It Could Matter More*, Templeton Press, West Conshohocken, PA, 2012.

Johnson, Robert, *Hard Time: Understanding and Reforming the Prison*, Monteray, CA, Brooks/Cole, 1987.

Kelly, Matthew, *The Dream Manager*, Hachette Books, N. Y., 2007.

Keller, Timothy, *Ministries of Mercy: The Call of the Jericho Road*, P & R Publishing, Phillipsburg, NJ, 2015.

Kerley, Kent R. *Religious Faith in Correctional Contexts*, First Forum Press, Boulder, CO, 2014.

Kimsey-House, Henry, Kimsey-House, Karen, Sandahl, Phillip and Whitworth, Laura, *Co-Active Coaching; Changing Business/ Transforming Lives*, Nichola Brealey Publishing, Boston, MA, 2011.

Kistemaker, Simon J., *Hebrews,* Libros Desafío, 2016.

Kuyper, Lester J., Grace and Truth: An Old Testament
Description of God, and it's use in the Johannine Gospel,
Interpretation: A Journal of Bible and Theology, Volume: 18,
issue: 1, January 1, 1964.

Landrigan, Kevin, *In NH, Pence says Trump tax cut is for the
forgotten,* New Hampshire Union Leader, March 22, 2018.

Lanigan, Tim, *Rebuilding Your Life: 12 Benefits of Christian
Redemption,* Palmetto Publishing Group, Charleston, SC,
2020. (The companion volume to the current book).

Latessa, Edward J., Homelessness and Reincarceration, *Criminology
and Public Policy,* Hoboken, (Mar 2004).

Lee, Morgan, Life After Prison, *Christianity Today,* Volume 60,
Number 7, Carol Stream, IL, September 2016.

Leonardson, John, and Anderson, John, *The Prison Bible,* World
Bible Translation Center, Bible League International, Fort
Worth, TX, 2013.

Lloyd-Jones, Martyn, *Joy Unspeakable: Power and Renewal in the
Holy Spirit,* Wheaton, IL: Harold Shaw Publishers, 1985.

Lupton, Robert D., *Compassion, Justice, and the Christian Life:
Rethinking Ministry to the Poor,* Gospel Light, Regal Books,
Ventura, CA, 2007.

Markway, Jeananne, and Worsham, Doug, The Potency of Faith in
Successful Offender Reentry, *Corrections Today;* Lanham
(Dec 2009).

Marsh, Charles, Dietrich Bonhoeffer, an essay within – David F. Ford, editor, The Modern Theologians, An Introduction to Christian Theology in the Twentieth Century, Malden, MA, Blackwell Publishers, 2001.

Martin, Curly, The Life Coaching Handbook: Everything You Need To Be An Effective Life Coach, Bethel, CT, Crown House Publishing, 2013.

Martinson, Robert, What Works? Questions and Answers About Prison Reform The Public Interest; New York, (Spring 1974).

Mays, James L., General Editor, Harper's Bible Commentary, Harper and Rowe, San Francisco, 1988.

McGowan, M. J., (2016). Location, Location, Mis-location: How local land use restrictions are dulling halfway housing's criminal rehabilitation potential. The Urban Lawyer, 48(2), 329-363. Retrieved from: http://0-search.proquest.com. library.regent.edu/docview/1826428307?accountid=13479

McNeal, Reggie, The Present Future: Six Tough Questions for the Church, San Francisco, CA, Jossey-Bass, 2003.

Menninger, Karl, The crime of Punishment, New York: The Viking Press, 1968.

Mitchell, S. D., (2011). IMPEDING REENTRY: AGENCY AND JUDICIAL OBSTACLES TO LONGER HALFWAY HOUSE PLACEMENTS. Michigan Journal of Race & Law, 16(2), 235-320, retrieved from: http://0search.proquest.com.library.regent.edu/ docview/1240345354?accountid=13479 (reference)

Morris, Betsy, "So You're a Player. Do You Need a Coach? *Fortune* 141, no.4, (February 2000).

Murray, Iain H., *D. Martin-Lloyd Jones: The First Forty Years 1899-1939*, Banner of Truth, Edinburgh, 1983.

Nolan, Pat, *When Prisoners Return,* Prison Fellowship, Merrifield, VA, 2004.

O'Brien, Peter T., *The Letter to the Hebrews* (Pillar New Testament Commentary), Eerdmans, 2010.

oxfordreference.com quick reference definition of *social justice.*

Packer, J. I., *Knowing God,* InterVarsity Press, Downers Grove, IL, 1973.

Patterson, Kerry, Grenny, Joseph, McMillan, Ron, Switzler, Al, *Crucial Conversations: Tools for Talking When Stakes are High.* New York, McGraw Hill, 2012.

Perkins, John M., *Restoring At – Risk Communities: Doing It Together & Doing It Right,* Grand Rapids, MI, Baker Books, 1995.

Polhill, John B., *Paul and His Letters,* Broadman and Holman Publishers, Nashville, TN, 1999.

Recovery Coach Academy, Connecticut Community for Addiction Recovery, July, 2019.

Robinson, George, *The Book of Isaiah in Fifteen Studies,* Hard Press, Miami FL, 2016.

Rogers, Donna, Reentry Programs that Make an Impact, *Corrections Forum*; Hicksville (Mar/Apr 2016).

Ross, Jeffrey Ian, and Richards, Stephen C., *Beyond Bars: Rejoining Society after Prison,* New York, Alpha Books/ Penguin Random House, 2009.

Ryrie, Charles C., *The Ryrie Study Bible (NKJV),* Moody Press, Chicago, IL, 1985.

Samuels, Charles, Director of the Bureau of Prisons, House Appropriations Subcommittee on Commerce, Justice, Science, and Related Agencies Hearing: FY2013 budget for the Bureau of Prisons. Congressional Documents and Publications; Washington, (Mar 6, 2012).

Scott, Susan, Fierce Conversations: Achieving Success at Work & in Life, One Conversation at a Time, New York, Berkley Publishing, 2004.

Seiter, Richard P., and Kadela, Karen R., *Prisoner Reentry: What Works, What Does Not, and What Is Promising, Sage* Journal, Volume: 49 issue: 3, July 1, 2003.

Sewell, Zach, *Prisoners in the Bible,* WestBow Press, Bloomington, IN, 2012.

Sider, Ronald J., *Doing Evangelism Jesus' Way: How Christians Demonstrate the Good News.* Evangel Publishing House, Nappanee, IN, 2003.

Smith, Harold B., Our Back-From-Prison Family, *Christianity Today,* Volume 60, Number 7, Carol Stream, IL, September 2016.

Soulen, Richard N., and Soulen, R. Kendall, Handbook of Biblical Criticism, Westminster John Knox Press, 2011.

Spitale, Lennie, *Prison Ministry,* (Nashville: Broadman and Holman, 2002.

Stoltzfus, Tony, *Coaching Questions: A Coaches Guide to Powerful Asking Skills,* Virginia Beach, VA, Lifeforming Institute, 2008.

Stoltzfus, Tony, *Leadership Coaching: The Disciplines, Skills, and Heart of a Christian Coach,* Booksurge, Virginia Beach, VA, 2005.

Strong, James, *Strong's Exhaustive Concordance of the Bible,* Crusade Bible Publishers Inc., Nashville, TN, circa 1975.

Sweeney, Marvin A., *Isaiah 40-66,* Eerdman's, Grand Rapids, MI, 2016.

The Sentencing Project: Fact Sheet: Trends in U.S. Corrections.

Tripp, Paul David, *Instruments in the Redeemer's Hands: People in Need of Change Helping People in Need of Change,* P & R Publishing, Phillipsburg, NJ, 2002.

Trulear, Harold Dean, Balancing Justice with Mercy: Creating a Healing Community, *Social Work and Christianity,* Botsford (Spring 2011).

Tuck, Willian Powell, *Authentic Evangelism: Sharing the Good News with Sense and Sensibility,* Judson Press, Valley Forge, PA, 2002.

Umidi, Joseph, senior editor, *Accelerated Coach Training Manual. TLC,* Virginia Beach, Lifeforming Institute, 2007.

Umidi, Joseph, *Transformational Coaching: Bridge Building That Impacts, Connects, and Advances the Ministry and the Marketplace,* Xulon Press, U.S., 2005.

Unger, Merrill Frederick, revised by Larson, Gary N., *The New Unger's Bible Handbook*, Moody Press, Chicago, IL, 1998.

U.S. Department of Justice, Office of Justice Programs, Bureau of Justice Statistics: Durose, Matthew R., Cooper, Alexia D., and Snyder, Howard N., *Recidivism of Prisoners Released in 30 States in 2005: Patterns from 2005 to 2010*, April, 2014.

Vianna, Fernando de Mello, Editor in Chief, *The American Heritage Desk Dictionary*, Boston, MA, Houghton-Mifflin, 1981.

Villafañe, Eldin, *Seek the Peace of the City: Reflections on Urban Ministry*, Eerdman's. Grand Rapids, MI, 1995.

Visher, Christy A., Returning Home: Emerging Findings and Policy Lessons about Prisoner Reentry, *Federal Sentencing Reporter*, FSR, New York, Vol. 20, No. 2 (December 2007).

Walmsey, Roy, *World Population List*, 10th ed. (Essex: International Centre for Prison Studies, 2013).

Wheeler, Darrell P., and Patterson, George, Prisoner Reentry, *Health & Social Work*; Oxford (May 2008).

Wilkinson, Bruce, *The Dream Giver: Following Your God-Given Destiny*, Multomah Books, Colorado Springs, CO, 2003.

Willard, Dallas, *The Divine Conspiracy: Rediscovering our Hidden Life in God*, New York, NY, Harper - Collins, 1997.

Young, Duane, and Judnick, Mike, Faith-Based Programming: Salvation to Reintegration, *American Jails*; Hagerstown (Jul/Aug 2012).

ENDNOTES

Introduction

1 Roy Walmsey, *World Population List*, 10th ed. (Essex: International Centre for Prison Studies, 2013).

2 https://www.sentencingproject.org/criminal-justice-facts/

3 E. A. Carson, and W. J. Sabol, (2012). *Prisoners in 2011.* Washington, D.C., Bureau of Justice Statistics; Mauer, M., and King, R. (2007). *A 25-Year Quagmire: The War on Drugs and its Impact on American Society.* Washington, D.C.: The Sentencing Project.

4 E. A. Carson, and D. Golinelli, (2013). *Prisoners in 2012.* Washington, D.C.: Bureau of Justice Statistics.

5 T. Bonczar, (2003). *Prevalence of Imprisonment in the U.S. Population, 1974-2001.* Washington, D.C.: Bureau of Justice Statistics.

6 *The Sentencing Project: Fact Sheet: Trends in U.S. Corrections,* 6.

7 U.S. Department of Justice, Office of Justice Programs, Bureau of Justice Statistics, (April 2014): Durose, Matthew R., Cooper, Alexia D., and Snyder, Howard N., *Recidivism of Prisoners Released in 30 States in 2005: Patterns from 2005 to 2010.*

8 Pat Nolan, *When Prisoners Return,* Prison Fellowship, Merrifield, VA, 2004, 24.

9 Mark P. Fisher, www.samekindofdifferentasmefoundation. org/blog/2018/2/24/7-practical-ways-we-can-help-some-one-experiencing-homelessness?

Chapter 1. The Yoke

10 F. C. Jennings, *Studies in Isaiah,* Wipf and Stock, Eugene, OR, 2001, pg. 677

11 oxfordreference.com quick reference definition of *social justice.*

Chapter 2. To Be a Christian Is to Have a Mission

12 The literary magnitude of the Book of Isaiah cannot be overstated. Writers of commentaries and biblical resources are effusive in their praise of this volume, and rightly so. The following are some examples:

Isaiah (Jehovah is salvation) is the great messianic prophet and prince of OT prophets (Unger, pg. 241).

Isaiah's place at the head of the prophetic books is well deserved. There is nothing to equal his tremendous vision of God and the glory in store for God's people until we reach John's book of Revelation, at the end of the New Testament. Other prophets came before him historically, but there was none greater (Alexander, pg. 376).

The book of Isaiah when treated as an organic whole is a grand masterpiece (Robinson, George, *The Book of Isaiah,* pg. 13).

Longer than any other prophetic book, it contains the fullest Messianic predictions to be found in the Old Testament, testifying in no uncertain way to "the sufferings of Christ, and the glory that should follow" (Ironside, H.A., *The Prophet Isaiah,* pg. 3).

13 The acts of compassion, justice and mercy which the passage under consideration speaks of is described by Walter Brueggemann as *neighborly attentiveness.* (*Isaiah 40-66,* pg. 191).

14 There is a parallel with verse 8 of Isaiah 58 seen in Isaiah 52:12b: "For the LORD will go before you, and the God of Israel will be your rear guard." (This term used as a phrase "rear guard" has the same root WORD meaning to gather together or harvest; in effect, "the LORD will keep you gathered close"). The phrase "Speaking wickedness" in verse 9 of Isaiah 58 has a parallel in Psalm 12: 2: "They speak idly everyone with his

neighbor; with flattering lips and a double heart they speak," and again in Psalm 10: 7; "His mouth is full of cursing and deceit and oppression; under his tongue is trouble and iniquity." Ah, *oppression* again. Trouble, iniquity, deceit, wickedness, and oppression appear to be birds of a feather.

15 Lloyd-Jones, *Joy Unspeakable,* pg. 80, and the following quote, pg.89

16 *Knowing God,* pg. 29

Chapter 3. Lovingkindness in Action

17 Typically, the first six verses of this last chapter in the epistle are connected as a segment. Segments or sections of the Bible are arranged-by study Bibles, Bible commentaries, and Bible handbooks- from general headings to specific descriptions. A symbolic metaphor for this arrangement can be seen in a Russian matryoshka doll, or babushka doll, which has several smaller dolls within it, in succession.

My Ryrie Study Bible sees chapter 11 as the beginning of:
"The Superiority of the Power of Christ,"
beginning with the subset "The Power of Faith in Christ" comprising;
"The Power of Hope in Christ" describing chapter 12;
and "The Power of the Love of Christ" indicating chapter 13.
As a further subset, Hebrews 13:1-6 are titled, *"In relation to social duties."*
(Ryrie, Charles, *The Ryrie Study Bible (NKJV),* pg. 1890).
Harper's Bible Commentary uses this breakdown:
"Christ, Faith, and Endurance" 12: 1-13
"Life in View of the End" 12:14 – 13:21
"Final Recommendations and Rhetorical Conclusion" 13:1-21
The subset 13: 1-6 is called *"Loving Service."*
(Mays, James, editor, *Harper's Bible Commentary,* pg. 1270)
The New Unger's Bible Handbook calls 13:1-6 *"The Expression of Faith in Daily Living."*

(Unger, Merrill F., The New Unger's Bible Handbook, pg. 603).
Simon Kistemaker calls 13:1-6 *"Communal Obligations." (Hebrews,* pg. 407)
James Draper calls 13:1-6 *"Marks of a Genuine Christian." (Hebrews, The Life That Pleases God,* pg. 361).
Peter T. O'Brien writes about 13:1-6, *"True Service to God Involves Serving His People"* (The Letter to the Hebrews (The Pillar New Testament Commentary), pg 504).
F. F. Bruce calls 13:1-6 *"Ethical Injunctions." (The Epistle to the Hebrews (The New International Commentary on the New Testament),* pg. 387).
Please forgive the frequency of these examples (and there are several others among the books spread out on my table). These were intended to demonstrate that the first six verses are generally grouped together. It is easy to recognize that the entire six verses have been put together as "social duties," or "communal obligations," or "ethical injunctions," but there is a further specificity seen in the first three verses taken as a pericope. Thankfully, there is at least one commentary which also groups these first three verses: *The Message of Hebrews* by Raymond Brown, part of *The Bible Speaks Today* series, with John R.W. Stott as series editor. In the commentary involving chapter 13, verses 1-3 are grouped in a section titled, "Be loving" (pg.248).

18 Historical - Cultural Background -- *Sitz im Leben* means "setting in life," used as a technical phrase in form criticism to refer to the "sociologic setting within the life of Israel or the early church." (Soulen and Soulen, *Handbook of Biblical Criticism,* pg. 187). What was the *Sitz im Leben* of the readers of the Book of Hebrews? Raymond Brown writes, "The appeal of some kind of Jewish Christian readership has been enhanced since the discovery of the Dead Sea Scrolls in the late 1940's, and some more recent scholars have suggested that the letter may have been sent initially to a first-century

Jewish group which held very similar views to those of the famous Qumran Community which treasured the scrolls and their teaching. The first readers were well acquainted with the Old Testament in its Greek version, the Septuagint. F.F. Bruce says that they might possibly have belonged to a first-century house church, but were at the same time part of 'the wider fellowship of a city church, and were tending to neglect the bond of fellowship that bound them to other Christians outside their own inner circle." (*The Message of the Hebrews,* pg. 16-17). We cannot be certain of the location of this group or church. Jerusalem, other places in Palestine, Alexandria, have all been considered. Raymond Brown feels "Rome is the most likely location." (Ibid, pg. 17). F.F. Bruce writes descriptively of the Greek philosopher Philo from Alexandria. He cites the Epistle to the Hebrews as the work of "another Alexandrian who… prefers the typology of salvation-history to Philonic allegory as the key to unlock the meaning of the Old Testament." (*New Testament History,* pg. 54). F. F. Bruce goes on to write of the Epistle to the Hebrews, "One of the most persuasive views of its purpose regards it as written to a 'house-church' or synagogue of Jewish Christians in Rome who found themselves out of sympathy with the prevalent trend of Roman Christianity, stimulated as it had been to fresh endeavor in the Gentile mission by Paul's recent stay in the city, and began to wonder if they might not have been too precipitate in committing themselves to a new order which involved an increasing breach with the cherished traditions of their old religion." (*New Testament History,* pg. 398).

19   Hebrews 13:1 Let brotherly love continue. Romans 12:10 uses the same term φιλαδελφία, as does 2 Peter 1:7. There are variations of this exhortation throughout scripture, especially seen in Leviticus 19:18, "…you shall love your neighbor as yourself…" and in John 15:12, "This is my commandment, that you love one another as I have loved you."

    Hebrews 13:2 Do not neglect to show hospitality to

BREAK EVERY YOKE

strangers, for by this some have entertained angels without knowing it.

There are frequent instances of hospitality throughout scripture: (Exo 22:21; 23:9; Lev 19:10,33,34; 24:22; Deu 10:18,19; 26:12,13; 27:19; Pro 9:1-5; 23:6-8; Isa 58:6,7; Mat 22:2-10; 25:34-46; Luk 14:12-14; Rom 12:13; 16:1,2; 1Ti 3:2; 5:10; Tit 1:7,8; Heb 13:2; 1Pe 4:9,11; 3Jo 1:5-8) to name a few. (*Nave's Topical Bible*). These instances almost all involve treatment of "the stranger." The sentiment expressed overall can be seen in Exodus 22:21, "You shall neither mistreat a stranger nor oppress him, for you were strangers in the land of Egypt" (NKJV). Hospitality to strangers remains a long-held tradition in the Middle-East, especially considering the hazards of travel through barren desert and open, hostile land. The tradition is honored by Muslims, borrowed from Hebrew tradition (and scriptures).

The latter phrase in this verse, ("by this some have entertained angels without knowing it"), could easily create many interesting theories. This writer's immediate sense is that this is the kind of a statement intended to be said with a wink in order to get a chuckle. It is exactly the kind of an "insider" reference (to the OT account of the angels that appeared to Abraham in Genesis 18 and Lot in Genesis 19) which the conscientious Jewish- Christian of the first century would be familiar with. *It is easy to imagine in this instance that the Book of Hebrews was indeed a written homily.*

20   DeSilva, David, *Perseverance in Gratitude*, pg. 485

21   In the *Pulpit Commentary*, we read, "The Hebrew readers have been also specially commended for their past sympathy with their imprisoned and despoiled brethren (Heb 10:33, etc.), having been themselves also at the same time persecuted. Whether or not sufferers themselves now, they must not be forgetful of those that are 'as bound with them' seems best taken as expressing the sympathy of one member with another." (http://biblehub.com/commentaries/pulpit/hebrews/13.htm).

22   http://biblehub.com/commentaries/gsb/hebrews/13.
htm

23   Friberg, *Analytical Greek Lexicon*, entry 25532: συνδεδεμένοι
- (pronounced "sundedemenoy") - a perfect passive nomina-
tive masculine plural participle verb from συνδέω, meaning: *to bind just as (i. e.* jointly with*) another*: perfect passive
participle ὡς συνδεδεμένοι, as fellow-prisoners (A. V. *as
bound with* them), Heb. 13:3 (συνδεδεμενος τῷ ὁινοχόω,
Josephus, Antiquities 2, 5, 3). συνδέω *bind (with)* or *im-
prison (with)* Hb 13:3. συνδέω pf. pass. συνδέδεμαι; only
passive in the NT; literally, of prisoners bound with the
same chains *be bound together with*; more generally *be fellow
prisoners, be in prison with* (HE 13.3). The term "bound" has
103 references, 65 in the OT, and 38 in the NT (as listed in
Strong's Exhaustive Concordance of the Bible. (Strong, James,
pg. 138-139).

24   Holladay, *Hebrew and Aramaic Lexicon of the OT,* note 665:
סירוּסאלן - ו particle conjunction ל particle preposition רסא
verb qal passive participle masculine plural absolute.

25   We have seen that the LORD emphasizes mercy in Isaiah
58:6, "Is this not the fast that I have chosen: to loose the
bonds of wickedness, to undo the heavy burdens, to let the
oppressed go free, and that you break every yoke?" *Matthew
Henry's Concise Commentary* states, *"The heavy yoke of sin and
oppression must be removed. As sin and sorrow dry the bones
and weaken the strongest human constitution; so the duties
of kindness and charity strengthen and refresh both body and
mind."* (http://biblehub.com/commentaries/mhc.isaiah/58.
htm). Ministering by counseling, mentoring, or coaching is
a practical attempt at kindness and charity. Prisons are not
necessarily "bonds of wickedness," but many prisoners are *in*
bonds of wickedness, stuck by the "cords of the yoke." To
minister to former prisoners is to help undo heavy burdens
that they may bear. Doing ministry can be a way of loosening
the bonds of wickedness; undoing heavy burdens; letting the
oppressed go free; and breaking some yokes.
      Oppression can be within as well as from without.

Isaiah 58:6 is a mirror image of Isaiah 61 just three chapters later, which Jesus reads from and applies to Himself in Luke 4:18: "He has sent Me to heal the brokenhearted, to proclaim liberty to the captives... to set at liberty those who are oppressed." These are the characteristics of *hesed* (Hebrew term), the lovingkindness of God. When you minister to others, you are an extension of God's lovingkindness.

Chapter 4. Prisoner Rehabilitation

26   Lennie Spitale, *Prison Ministry*, (Nashville: Broadman and Holman, 2002), 127

27   Jeffrey Ian Ross and Stephen C. Richards, *Beyond Bars: Rejoining Society after Prison*, New York, Alpha Books/ Penguin Random House, 2009, xi, and the following quote, xii.

28   Jeffrey Ian Ross and Stephen C. Richards, *Beyond Bars: Rejoining Society after Prison*, New York, Alpha Books/ Penguin Random House, 2009, ix-xiii.

29   Lois G. Forer, *A Rage to Punish*, New York, NY, W. W. Norton & Company, 1994, 148, and the next quote, pg. 149.

30   Robert Johnson, *Hard Time: Understanding and Reforming the Prison*, Monteray, CA, Brooks/ Cole, 1987, 184, and following quotes, 182 twice, 183.

31   Karl Menninger, *The crime of Punishment*, New York: The Viking Press, 1968, 190.

32   Francis A. Allen, *Criminal Justice, Legal Values, and the Rehabilitative Ideal*, from Jeffrie G. Murphy, editor, *Punishment and Rehabilitation*, Belmont, California, Wadsworth Publishing Company, 1985, 182.

33   DeRosia, Victoria R., *Living Inside Prison Walls: Adjustment Behavior*, Westport, CT, Praeger Publishers, 1998, 172, as well as the next quote.

34   Richard Bovan, *10 Rules for Making it in Society After Doing Time: The Dedicated Ex-Prisoner's Guide to Life and Success on the Outside*, Memphis, TN, Full Surface Publishing, 2009, 11, and following quote, 42.

35   Demico Booth, *Getting Out & Staying Out: A Black Man's Guide to Success After Prison*, Memphis, TN, Full Surface Publishing, 2012, pg. 22 (and mentioned in Richard Bovan, *10 Rules for Making it in Society After Doing Time: The Dedicated Ex-Prisoner's Guide to Life and Success on the Outside*, Memphis, TN, Full Surface Publishing, 2009, 46.

36   Demico Booth, *Getting Out & Staying Out: A Black Man's Guide to Success After Prison*, Memphis, TN, Full Surface Publishing, 2012, 22.

37   Jimmy Carter, *Faith: A Journey for All*, Simon and Schuster, New York, 2018, 9, and the next two quotes, 11 and 9 again.

Chapter 5. Reentry

38   Chuck Colsen, with Anne Morse, *My Final Word: Holding Tight to the Issues that Matter Most*, Zondervan, Grand Rapids, MI, 2017, 183, as well as the following block quote.

39   Kent R. Kerley, *Religious Faith in Correctional Contexts*, First Forum Press, Boulder, CO, 2014, 1, and next quote, 2.

40   Kent R. Kerley, *Religious Faith in Correctional Contexts*, First Forum Press, Boulder, CO, 2014, 6, with the next quote 163. His second chapter, "The Relationship Between Religion and Criminal Behavior," includes more than thirty research studies. The results of these studies vary from positive to negative or mixed as regards the impact of religion upon crime. Each study is unique, and the issues are complex.

41   Byron R. Johnson, *More God, Less Crime: Why Faith Matters and How It Could Matter More*, Templeton Press, West Conshohocken, PA, 2012, (paperback), 78, and following five quotes, xii, 208, 185-186.

42   John Leonardson and John Anderson, *The Prison Bible*, World Bible Translation Center, Bible League International, Fort Worth, TX, 2013, A102.

43   Robert D. Lupton, *Compassion, Justice, and the Christian Life: Rethinking Ministry to the Poor*, Gospel Light, Regal Books, Ventura, CA, 2007, 69, as well as the next quote.

44   Louis B. Cei, Faith-Based Programs are Low-Cost Ways to Reduce Recidivism, *Corrections Today*; **Lanham** (Aug 2010): 48-51.

45   Richard P. Seiter, Karen R. Kadela, *Prisoner Reentry: What Works, What Does Not, and What Is Promising*, Sage Journal, Volume: 49 issue: 3, July 1, 2003, pg. 360-388. As sighted by: Darrell P. Wheeler and George Patterson, Prisoner Reentry, *Health & Social Work*; **Oxford** (May 2008): 145-7.

46   Laurie C. Bright, Mary G. Graham, Faith-Based Programs Give facilities a Helping Hand, *Corrections Today*, Lanham Vol. 69, Iss. 5, (Oct. 2007): 137-139, as well as the following quote.

47   Harold Dean Trulear, Balancing Justice with Mercy: Creating a Healing Community, *Social Work and Christianity*; **Botsford** (Spring 2011): 74-87.

48   Jeananne Markway and Doug Worsham, The Potency of Faith in Successful Offender Reentry, *Corrections Today*; **Lanham** (Dec 2009): 98-99.

49   Duane Young and Mike Judnick consider the status of recent decades of faith and prison life and acknowledge that, "The spiritual path and the path of positive behavior change did not always overlap." Their view of faith-based programs in prison is that of providing comfort to the prisoner, while not necessarily bringing about substantial rehabilitation. Young and Judnick are pointing out the need for actual transformation of the prisoner who will also be released into communities. These authors are acknowledging that rehabilitation should be emphasized throughout the period of incarceration; that if it is put off until release from prison, it is too late. "In concert with questions of faith are those of what to do about the growing jail and prison populations. Because 95 percent of all prisoners are eventually released into society (Gibbons & Katzenbach, 2006), it becomes even more important to adequately prepare those making their reentry into society." This figure of 95% being released is memorable, together with Johnson's account of two thou-

sand inmates being released every day! Duane Young and Mike Judnick, Faith-Based Programming: Salvation to Reintegration, *American Jails*; Hagerstown (Jul/Aug 2012): 30-32. Author's note [Gibbons, J. J., & Katzenbach, N.dB. (2006). Confronting confinement: A report of the Commission on Safety and Abuse in America's Prisons. Washington, D.C.: Vera Institute of Justice].

50   Donna Rogers, Reentry Programs that Make an Impact, *Corrections Forum*; **Hicksville** (Mar/Apr 2016): 15-16,18,20, including the next quote.

51   S. E. Costanza, Stephen M. Cox, John C. Kilburn, The Impact of Halfway Houses on Parole Success and Recidivism, *Journal of Sociological Research*, ISSN 1948-5468, 2015, Vol. 6, No. 2.

52   Pat Nolan, *When Prisoners Return*, Prison Fellowship, Merrifield, VA, 2004, xi, and the next quote, pg. 21.

Chapter 6. The Lord and the Prisoner

53   Fernando de Mello Vianna, Editor in Chief, *The American Heritage Desk Dictionary*, Boston, MA, Houghton-Mifflin, 1981, 960.

54   James Strong, *Strong's Exhaustive Concordance of the Bible*, Crusade Bible Publishers, Inc., Nashville, TN, 1990, Strong's' reference 2617.

55   Strong's' reference 0571.

56   Strong's' reference 5485.

57   Lester J. Kuyper, Grace and Truth: An Old Testament Description of God, and it's use in the Johannine Gospel, *Interpretation: A Journal of Bible and Theology*, Volume: 18, issue: 1, January 1, 1964, 3-19.

58   Iulian Faraonu, Divine Mercy in the Holy Bible, *Romanian Journal of Artistic Creativity*; Woodside, Vol. 4, Iss. 3, (Autumn 2016): 43-53. (Faraonu quotes Eleos R. Bultmann, *Theological dictionary of the* New Testament, vol 2. Kittel G, ed. Grand Rapids: Eerdmans, 1982).

59 Iulian Faraonu, Divine Mercy in the Holy Bible, *Romanian Journal of Artistic Creativity;* Woodside, Vol. 4, Iss. 3, (Autumn 2016): 43-53.

60 Zach Sewell, *Prisoners in the Bible,* WestBow Press, Bloomington, IN, 2012, xiii.

61 Strong's' reference 1004.

62 Strong's' reference 0615.

63 Strong's' reference 7617.

64 Strong's' reference 7628.

65 Strong's' reference 5650.

66 Strong's' reference 1198.

67 Strong's' reference 1401.

68 Strong's' reference 1249.

69 Strong's reference 8333 and 8331.

70 Strong's reference 4147.

71 Strong's reference 2131.

72 Strong's reference 0246.

73 Strong's reference 2397.

74 Strong's reference 254.

75 Strong's reference 3976.

76 Strong's reference 1199.

77 Strong's reference 1201.

78 Strong's reference 1210.

79 Strong's reference 1004.

Chapter 7. Life at Halfway Houses

80 https://www.nh.gov/nhdoc/divisions/community/calument.html

81 Andrew M. Colman. "halfway house." In *A Dictionary of Psychology*: Oxford University Press, 2015.

82 *Britannica Academic*, s.v. "Halfway house," accessed January 8, 2017, http://0-academic.eb.com.library.regent.edu/levels/collegiate/article/603888

83 M. J. McGowan (2016). Location, Location, Mis-location: How local land use restrictions are dulling halfway housing's

criminal rehabilitation potential. *The Urban Lawyer,* 48(2), 329-363. Retrieved from http://0-search.proquest.com.library.regent.edu/docview/1826428307?accountid=13479

84   *Britannica Academic,* s.v. "Halfway house," as with the next quote.

85   M. J. McGowan (2016). Location, location, mis-location: How local land use restrictions are dulling halfway housing's criminal rehabilitation potential. *The Urban Lawyer,* 48(2), 329-363, and the following quote.

86   Welcoming prisoners post release has not been an overwhelming trend. "But most community-release advocates ultimately faltered in the face of popular and political uneasiness about convicts behind functionally-unlocked doors. By the Great Depression, according to one source, only one halfway home remained open in the United States: a charity-funded facility in Pittsburgh, Pennsylvania."

87   *Britannica Academic,* s.v. "Halfway house," including the next three quotes.

88   Sylvia L. Golomb and Andrea Kocsis, *The Halfway House: On the Road To Independence,* Brunner/ Mazel, Inc., New York, 1988, vii, and the next quote, xi.

89   M. J. McGowan (2016). Location, location, mis-location: How local land use restrictions are dulling halfway housing's criminal rehabilitation potential. *The Urban Lawyer,* 48(2), 329-363. Retrieved (together with the next two quotes) from   http://0search.proquest.com.library.regent.edu/docview/1826428307?accountid=13479

90   Robert Martinson, What Works? Questions and Answers About Prison Reform **The Public Interest; New York** (Spring 1974): 22.

91   M. J. McGowan (2016). Location, Location, Mis-location: How local land use restrictions are dulling halfway housing's criminal rehabilitation potential. *The Urban Lawyer,* 48(2), 329-363. Retrieved from http://0-search.proquest.com.library.regent.edu/docview/1826428307?accountid=13479

92   S. D. Mitchell (2011). IMPEDING REENTRY: AGENCY

AND JUDICIAL OBSTACLES TO LONGER HALFWAY HOUSE PLACEMENTS. *Michigan Journal of Race & Law, 16*(2), 235-320, together with the following two quotes, Retrieved from http://0-search.proquest.com.library.regent.edu/docview/1240345354?accountid=13479 (reference)

93   M. J. McGowan (2016). Location, Location, Mis-location: How local land use restrictions are dulling halfway housing's criminal rehabilitation potential. *The Urban Lawyer, 48*(2), 329-363, and the next quote.

94   Kent R. Kerley, *Religious Faith in Correctional Contexts,* First Forum Press, Boulder, CO, 2014, 16.

95   Byron R. Johnson, *More God, Less Crime: Why Faith Matters and How It Could Matter More*, Templeton Press, West Conshohocken, PA, 2012, (paperback), 189-190, and the next three quotes, 191, 191-192, 192-193.

96   Edward J. Latessa, Homelessness and Reincarceration, *Criminology and Public Policy,* Hoboken, (Mar 2004): 137-138, and the next quote.

97   Anonymous, *Office of Justice Programs – U. S. Department of Justice; Justice Department Announces Grants Under Second Chance Act Prisoner Reentry Initiative*, Mental Health Weekly Digest; Atlanta, 19 Oct 2009: 170.

98   Christy A. Visher, Returning Home: Emerging Findings and Policy Lessons about Prisoner Reentry, *Federal Sentencing Reporter,* FSR, New York, Vol. 20, No. 2 (December 2007), 100.

99   S. D. Mitchell (2011). IMPEDING REENTRY: AGENCY AND JUDICIAL OBSTACLES TO LONGER HALFWAY HOUSE PLACEMENTS. *Michigan Journal of Race & Law, 16*(2), 235-320, together with the next quote.

100   *Britannica Academic*, s.v. "Halfway House."

101   Charles Samuels, Director of the Bureau of Prisons, House Appropriations Subcommittee on Commerce, Justice, Science, and Related Agencies Hearing: FY2013 budget for the Bureau of Prisons. Congressional Documents and Publications; Washington, (Mar 6, 2012), and the next quote.

102   J. Davidson (2016). *Report: Halfway house issues mean high-risk offenders could be released too soon.* Washington: WP Company LLC d/b/a The Washington Post. Retrieved (with the following three quotes) from http://0-search.proquest.com.library.regent.edu/docview/1841309707?accountid=13479

103   S.D. Mitchell, (2011). IMPEDING REENTRY: AGENCY AND JUDICIAL OBSTACLES TO LONGER HALFWAY HOUSE PLACEMENTS. *Michigan Journal of Race & Law, 16*(2), 235-320.

104   J. Davidson, (2016). *Report: Halfway house issues mean high-risk offenders could be released too soon.*

Chapter 8. Life Coaching

105   Emmy van Deurzen and Monica Hanaway, editors, *Existential Perspectives on Coaching,* Palgrave MacMillan, Hampshire, England, 2012, xv.

106   Gary R. Collins, *Christian Coaching,* Colorado Springs, CO, NavPress, 2009, 12.

107   Emmy van Deurzen and Monica Hanaway, editors, *Existential Perspectives on Coaching,* Palgrave MacMillan, Hampshire, England, 2012, xv, together with the following quote.

108   Joseph Umidi, ed., *Accelerated Coach Training Manual, TLC* (Virginia Beach, Lifeforming Institute, 2007), 275.

109   Gary R. Collins, *Christian Coaching,* Colorado Springs, CO, NavPress, 2009, 12.

110   Gary R. Collins, *Christian Coaching,* Colorado Springs, CO, NavPress, 2009, 13, according to Betsy Morris, "So You're a Player. Do You Need a Coach? Fortune 141, no.4, (February 2000): 144-145.

111   Gary R. Collins, *Christian Coaching,* 14, and the three next quotes, 14, 22, 23.

112   Paul David Tripp, *Instruments in the Redeemer's Hands: People in Need of Change Helping People in Need of Change,* P & R Publishing, Phillipsburg, NJ, 2002, 18, and next quote, 19.

113   For the writing team of Patterson et al., coaching conversa-
        tions are crucial. They write, "Our research has shown that
        strong relationships, careers, organizations, and communi-
        ties all draw from the same source of power – the ability
        to talk openly about high stakes, emotional, controversial
        topics." Kerry Patterson, Joseph Grenny, Ron McMillan, Al
        Switzler, *Crucial Conversations: Tools for Talking When the
        Stakes are High,* McGraw-Hill, New York, 2012, 9. Patterson
        et al. makes what is referred to as both "our audacious claim"
        and "The Law of Crucial Conversations:" "Twenty years of
        research involving more than 100,000 people reveals that
        the key skill of effective leaders, team-mates, parents, and
        loved ones is the capacity to skillfully address emotionally
        and politically risky issues. Period." (pg. 9-19). What this
        team of writers is reinforcing is the truly crucial, vitally im-
        portant nature of an intentional, thought-out conversation
        with a person in need. Life coaching, when applied well and
        properly during the time of transition that the halfway house
        represents, has value, has great potential to be pivotal in the
        lives of the people in them who are hoping to rebuild their
        lives. They are living in a high-stakes environment, where
        going back to prison is a real possibility. It is a time of great
        vulnerability, and there are also emotional and controversial
        topics to consider.
            An article written by Susan Cavanagh of the *Edmonton
        Journal* from the province of Alberta, Canada, discusses a May
        2014 presentation at the Giovanni Concert Hall, attended by
        government representatives, business and church leaders: "the
        group included the chaplaincy of the Edmonton Institute for
        Women, concerned people from West Edmonton Christian
        Assembly and a volunteer ministry known as No More
        Leftovers." (Susan Cavanagh, Adopt1, *Edmunton Journal,*
        Edmunton, Alberta, Canada, 17 May 2014: F.14). In her ar-
        ticle, Cavanagh expresses the rhetorical question: "If we don't
        start helping inmates with transformational change long be-
        fore they leave prison, how do you think they will come out?"

Cavanagh is specifically speaking to the needs of a local women's prison as she writes

No More Leftovers is a team of trained volunteers who coach at the women's prison every week, showing inmates how to integrate what they're learning. And for those who have been approved, we are able to take them to church each week. Besides experiencing the lifechanging value of church services, these inmates meet a new group of people long before parole and discharge. Between the coaching and church attendance, we have witnessed signs of tremendous transformation... We asked the halfway house leaders in our city how many churches were showing up at their doorstep to help take women to church each week. Their answer? Zero.

This single newspaper article combines a focus upon rehabilitation and re-integration, with life coaching, having high regard for lifechanging with the involvement of the church, and a direct connection with halfway houses!

114   Life coaching seeks the transformation of the lives of people who have been shut away. Dietrich Bonhoeffer was shut away in Flossenburg prison, Germany, from 1943 until he was executed in 1945. In *Letters and Papers from Prison*, he states, "it is only when one loves life and the world so much that without them everything would be gone, that one can believe in the resurrection and a new world."(Charles Marsh, *Dietrich Bonhoeffer*, an essay within – David F. Ford, editor, *The Modern Theologians, An Introduction to Christian Theology in the Twentieth Century*, Malden, MA, Blackwell Publishers, 2001, 48).Bonhoeffer was a deep-thinking theologian, but experienced the loneliness and despair of a prisoner. He speaks of embracing that which has been taken away, and the importance of faith in Him who was resurrected. Bonhoeffer's plaintive statement represents a backdrop against which Christians should consider ministering to the former prisoner and the homeless.

115   Henry Kimsey-House, Karen Kimsey-House, Phillip Sandahl, and Laura Whitworth, *Co-Active Coaching; Changing Business/ Transforming Lives,* Nichola Brealey Publishing, Boston, MA, 2011, 15, and next quote, 19.

116   Coaches should also be aware that they are having an impact upon clients and become "vigilant self-monitors."Kerry Patterson, Joseph Grenny, Ron McMillan, Al Switzler, *Crucial Conversations: Tools for Talking When Stakes are High.* New York, McGraw Hill, 2012, 63.

117   Susan Scott, *Fierce Conversations: Achieving Success at Work & in Life, One Conversation at a Time,* New York, Berkley Publishing, 2004, xv.

118   Curley Martin, *The Life Coaching Handbook: Everything You Need To Be An Effective Life Coach,* Bethel, CT, Crown House Publishing, 2013, 70, and the next quote, 5.

119   "Transformation Happens Experientially – The things that most deeply shape us happen through experiences and relationships, not by accumulating information. Therefore, transformational coaching focuses on engaging the teachable moments of life in the context of a transparent coaching relationship to produce lasting change." Tony Stoltzfus, *Leadership Coaching: The Disciplines, Skills, and Heart of a Christian Coach,* Booksurge, Virginia Beach, VA, 2005, 75.

120   Jane Creswell addresses the process of transformation and renewal by stating, "Coaching focuses on promoting discovery. *Christ-Centered* coaching additionally utilizes the power of the Holy Spirit in that discovery process." (Jane Creswell, *Christ-Centered Coaching: 7 Benefits for Ministry,* (St. Louis, MO, Chalice Press, 2006), 13).Creswell makes frequent reference to the phrase "untapped potential": "By helping you focus on the untapped potential within you, a coach can guide you to discover that potential and what needs to be done." (Ibid),

      These concepts of discovery and bringing out potential are also mentioned in the book *Primal Leadership,* although this book is written by and for people in the corporate world. Author Daniel Goleman observes, "What organizations everywhere need now is to realize the benefits of primal leadership by cultivating leaders who generate the emotional resonance that lets people flourish. Daniel Goleman, Richard Boyzatzis, Annie McKee, Annie, *Primal Leadership: Unleashing the Power of Emotional Intelligence,* (Boston, MA, Harvard Business School Press, 2013), xv.

Coaching helps people to flourish. Tony Stoltzfus affirms, "Paul [the apostle] was all about unleashing people and making them into fully developed leaders... Paul's objective was to raise up robust, mature believers who knew how to chew the meat of responsibility. Coaching mirrors that approach: it is more interested in building capable, responsible adults than in feeding people solutions to immediate problems." (Tony Stoltzfus, *Leadership Coaching: The Disciplines, Skills, and Heart of a Christian Coach,* (Virginia Beach, VA, Lifeforming Institute, 2005), 39-40). Tony Stoltzfus uses dating and marriage as a metaphor for coaching in ministry practice: "you don't marry a person's past. You don't keep a scorecard and rank your dates based on how many mistakes they made before you met: you fall in love with who someone is. You love their identity, their 'being,' not their track record." (Ibid., 63). This is just like our relationship with Jesus, Who, after all, is our model for not only doing ministry, but for living itself.

121 Gary R. Collins, *Christian Coaching,* Colorado Springs, CO, NavPress, 2009, 171.

122 "We can be pushed down the road by deadlines and expectations and to-do lists. We can be driven by the desire for money or accomplishment or by the promises we make. Or we can be pulled down the road by the gravitational force of a compelling vision, like water running downhill." Henry Kimsey-House, Karen Kimsey-House, Phillip Sandahl, and Laura Whitworth, *Co-Active Coaching; Changing Business/ Transforming Lives,* Nichola Brealey Publishing, Boston, MA, 2011, 25.

123 Joseph Umidi, *Transformational Coaching: Bridge Building*

That Impacts, Connects, and Advances the Ministry and the Marketplace, (City: State needed here: Xulon Press, 2005), 24. The coach listens beyond the daydreams and self-centered dreams to what Dr. Umidi refers to 'core dreams': "When we hear those core dreams in another, we can be their advocates to call them forth in the stewardship of their own lives." (Ibid., pg.25).

124 Tony Stoltzfus, *Leadership Coaching: The Disciplines, Skills, and Heart of a Christian Coach,* (Virginia Beach, VA, Lifeforming Institute, 2005), 52.

125 Matthew Kelly, *The Dream Manager,* Hachette Books, N. Y., 2007, 82.

126 Bruce Wilkinson, *The Dream Giver: Following Your God-Given Destiny,* Multnomah Books, Colorado Springs, CO, 2003, 156, and next quote, 8.

127 Mark Batterson, *The Circle Maker: Praying Dreams Around Your Biggest Dreams and Greatest Fears,* Zondervan, Grand Rapids, MI, 2011, 44, with the next two quotes, 85.

128 Curly Martin, *The Life Coaching Handbook: Everything You Need To Be An Effective Life Coach,* Crown House, Bethel, CT, 2013, v., and next quote, 9.

129 Joseph Umidi, *Transformational Coaching: Bridge Building That Impacts, Connects, and Advances the Ministry and the Marketplace,* (U.S.: Xulon Press, 2005), 28.

130 The *Lifeforming Leadership Coaching* manual includes information about helping to identify "dreambusters:" "Sometimes talking about dreambusters will open up a whole can of worms – past hurts, lies, insecurities, etc. that together make up a fairly major challenge. Don't hesitate to step back from the dreaming process and focus on the topic at hand when you discover a deeper issue." Doug Fike, Tony Stoltzfus, D. Lyn Eichman, *Lifeforming Leadership Coaching, Life Focus Track,* (Virginia Beach, Lifeforming Institute, 2008), 32.

131 Tony Evans, *Discover Your Destiny: Let God Use You Like He Made You,* Harvest House, Eugene, OR, 2013, 85-86.

132 Eldin Villafañe, *Seek the Peace of the City: Reflections on*

Urban Ministry, Eerdman's. Grand Rapids, MI, 1995, 2.

133   Tony Evans, *Discover Your Destiny: Let God Use You Like He Made You,* Harvest House, Eugene, OR, 2013, 12, and next quote, 13.

134   John Leonardson and John Anderson, *The Prison Bible,* World Bible Translation Center, Bible League International, Fort Worth, TX, 2013, A77, and following quote, A94.

135   Robert E. Coleman, *The Master Plan of Evangelism,* Fleming H. Revell Co., Grand Rapids, MI, 1993, 99.

136   These questions are universal, yet many were included in: Doug Fike, Tony Stoltzfus, D. Lyn Eichman, *Lifeforming Leadership Coaching, Life Focus Track,* (Virginia Beach, Lifeforming Institute, 2008).

Chapter 9. Compassionate Evangelism

137   Dallas Willard, *The Divine Conspiracy: Rediscovering our Hidden Life in God,* New York, NY, Harper - Collins, 1997, 306.

138   Charles Colson, with Ellen Santilli Vaughn, *The Body: Being Light in Darkness,* Dallas, TX, Word Publishing, 1992, 86, and the next quote, 334.

139   Reggie McNeal, *The Present Future: Six Tough Questions for the Church,* San Francisco, CA, Jossey-Bass, 2003, 9.

140   John M. Perkins, *Restoring At – Risk Communities: Doing It Together & Doing It Right,* Grand Rapids, MI, Baker Books, 1995, 89.

141   Larry Crabb, *Becoming a True Spiritual Community: A Profound Vision of What the Church Can Be,* Nashville, TN, Thomas Nelson, 1999, 180.

142   Antipas L. Harris, *Holy Spirit, Holy Living: Toward a Practical Theology of Holiness for Twenty-First Century Churches,* Eugene, Oregon, Wipf & Stock, 2013, 160.

143   Kim Hammond and Darren Cronshaw, *Sentness: Six Postures of Missional Christians,* Downer Grove, IL, InterVarsity Press, 2014, 119, and the next quote, 119-120.

144   Robert E. Coleman, *The Master Plan of Evangelism,* 9, and

BREAK EVERY YOKE

next quote, 14.

145   Ronald J. Sider, *Doing Evangelism Jesus' Way: How Christians Demonstrate the Good News*. Evangel Publishing House, Nappanee, IN, 2003, 13, and three following quotes, 78, 84, 86.

146   William Powell Tuck, *Authentic Evangelism: Sharing the Good News with Sense and Sensibility*, Judson Press, Valley Forge, PA, 2002, xii, and the two next quotes, 19, 20.

147   Robert D. Lupton, *Compassion, Justice, and the Christian Life: Rethinking Ministry to the Poor*, Gospel Light, Regal Books, Ventura, CA, 2007, 126.

148   Timothy Keller, *Ministries of Mercy: The Call of the Jericho Road*, P & R Publishing, Phillipsburg, NJ, 2015, 31, and the two next quotes from pg. 117.

149   Jimmy Carter, *Faith: A Journey for All*, Simon and Schuster, New York, 2018, 90.

150   J. I. Packer, *Knowing God*, InterVarsity Press, Downers Grove, IL, 1973, 62.

151   Mark E. Dever, *The Gospel and personal Evangelism*, Crossway Books, Wheaton, IL, 2007, 42, and two following quotes, 42, 51.

152   Iain H. Murray, *D. Martin-Lloyd Jones: The First Forty Years 1899-1939*, Banner of Truth, Edinburgh, 1983, 246.

153   In the foreword to *The Power of Cooperative Evangelism*, Robert E. Coleman writes, "evangelism becomes the heartbeat of our ministry to the world. Other expressions of our witness are necessary, of course. But proclaiming by word and deed the good news of redeeming grace is the most crucial. Indeed, introducing persons to Jesus brings the church into existence, and apart from this practice, the church would soon become extinct." (Dr. Robert O. Ferm, edited by Dr. Tom Phillips, *The Power of Cooperative Evangelism*, EMIS (Evangelism and Missions Information Service), Wheaton, IL, 2002, 11, and the next quote, 20). The author, Dr. Robert O. Ferm, makes this powerful statement: "Once evangelism is understood, we can see it is the foundational function of the Church of Christ." The emphasis

of this book, originally published in 1958, is cooperative evangelism among denominations. Christianity is less territorial now in the twenty-first century. At Helping Hands Outreach Center, there is a partnering ministry in the building which takes up a couple of rooms, an office and a storage room for clothing to be distributed. It is known as Christian Aftercare Ministry, which serves former prisoners. There is no denominational emphasis between the ministries. Helping Hands has a director, drug counselors, and a chaplain. There are a pair of volunteers with Christian Aftercare Ministry. Every Christian in the building, including residents, encourages church attendance in the area. But there is no expressed preference for a denomination. There are a couple of churches known of for their outreach to former inmates, and these locations are given honorable mentions.

154   Morgan Lee, Life After Prison, *Christianity Today,* Volume 60, Number 7, Carol Stream, IL, September 2016, 41, and the following quote, 43.

155   Harold B. Smith, Our Back-From-Prison Family, *Christianity Today,* Volume 60, Number 7, Carol Stream, IL, September 2016, 49, and next quote, 51.

156   Jim Buchan, *Apostolic Evangelism,* Firewind, Mansfield, PA, 2001, 19.

Chapter 10. A Heart for the Homeless of the City

157   Jack Dennison, *City Reaching – On the Road to Community Transformation,* William Carey Library, Pasadena, CA, 1999, 259.

158   (In the Forward to) Eldin Villafane, *Seek the Peace of the City: Reflections on Urban Ministry,* Eerdmans, Grand Rapids, MI, 1995, xii.

159   Mark Hayward, *Homeless tents demolished Camps in the crosshairs 1 homeless enclave bulldozed, 2 others eyed,* Manchester

Union Leader, New Hampshire Sunday News, April 8th, Vol. 72, No. 27, front page.

160 Paul Feeley, *President praises Safe Station, calls it 'really quite incredible.'* New Hampshire Union Leader, March 19, 2018.

161 Kevin Landrigan, *In NH, Pence says Trump tax cut is for the forgotten,* New Hampshire Union Leader, March 22, 2018.

162 Robert D. Lupton, *Compassion, Justice, and the Christian Life: Rethinking Ministry to the Poor,* Gospel Light, Regal Books, Ventura, CA, 2007, 38, and three following quotes, 39, 38, 38.

163 http://www.gordonconwell.edu/boston/Meet-Our-Staff.cfm

164 Eldin Villafañe, *Seek the Peace of the City: Reflections on Urban Ministry,* Eerdman's. Grand Rapids, MI, 1995, 1, and next two quotes, 2, 3.

Chapter 11. Recovery

165 *Recovery Coach Academy,* Connecticut Community for Addiction Recovery, July, 2019.

Chapter 12. All Hands On Deck

166 Tim Lanigan, *Rebuilding Your Life: 12 Benefits of Christian Redemption,* Palmetto Publishing Group, Charleston, SC. (The companion volume to the current book).

History to Reflect Upon Prisoners on the Old Testament

167 Bill T. Arnold, Bryan E. Beyer, *Encountering the Old Testament: A Christian Survey,* Baker Books, Grand Rapids, MI, 1999, 184.

168 Merrill Frederick Unger, revised by Gary N. Larson, *The New Unger's Bible Handbook,* Moody Bible Institute, Chicago, 1998, 181, and next two quotes, 182, 247.

169 James L. Mays, General Editor, *Harper's Bible Commentary,* Harper and Rowe, San Francisco, 1988, 557, and the fol-

lowing two quotes, 590, 637.

170   Fernando de Mello Vianna, Editor in Chief, *The American Heritage Desk Dictionary*, Houghton Mifflin Company, Boston, 1981, 614.

171   Merrill Frederick Unger, revised by Gary N. Larson, *The New Unger's Bible Handbook*, Moody Bible Institute, Chicago, 1998, 294.

172   David Alexander and Pat Alexander, editors, *Eerdmans' Handbook to the Bible*, William B. Eerdmans Publishing Co., Grand rapids, MI, 1976, 435.

173   Zach Sewell, *Prisoners in the Bible*, West Bow Press, Bloomington, IN, 2012, 43, and the next quote.

Prisoners in the New Testament

174   James L. Mays, General Editor, *Harper's Bible Commentary*, Harper and Rowe, San Francisco, 1988, 992.

175   Zach Sewell, *Prisoners in the Bible*, West Bow Press, Bloomington, IN, 2012, 68-69.

176   John B. Polhill, *Paul and His Letters*, Broadman and Holman Publishers, Nashville, TN, 1999, 332.

ABOUT THE AUTHOR

Dr. Tim Lanigan has a Bachelor of Science degree from Northeastern University, a Master of Divinity degree from Gordon-Conwell Theological Seminary, is a member of the Phi Alpha Chi Honor Society, and has a Doctor of Ministry degree from Regent University. He is an ordained Minister of the Gospel through IAM Minister's Fellowship (International Accelerated Missions) and has been to eleven countries on mission trips. He was on the board of directors for the *Doorway to Peace* ministry in Haiti, which established a grammar school, medical clinic and church. He was part of the *Authentic Christian Man* chapel ministry at the Concord, NH, men's prison for fifteen years and has done life coaching and evangelism at the Calumet Halfway House in Manchester, NH. He currently serves as Associate Pastor for the 1269 Café homeless outreach and as Chaplain for the Helping Hands Outreach transitional housing unit with 35 beds. Chaplain Tim is a drummer with a worship team, a certified Life Coach, and a trained Recovery Coach. He and his wife Yvonne, having four grown children and four grandkids, enjoy skiing in the Winter and paddle-boarding in the Summer.

Please consider reading the companion book to this volume –

Rebuilding Your Life: 12 Benefits of Christian Redemption
The action plans, steps, and discussion questions of the 14 sessions of this teaching program are intended to encourage the reader and anyone they would help, as either a supplement or as an alternative to 12 step programs.

Made in United States
North Haven, CT
25 January 2023

31618707R00134